HERE'S WH

RACHAEL ADAMS AND
EVERYDAY PRAYERS FOR LOVE...

In *Everyday Prayers for Love*, Rachael does a beautiful job of bringing us biblical and practical ways to grow in love, walk in love, and love others deeply. Love can be difficult to live out at times because we'll never measure up to Jesus's great love for us. But through stories, verses, questions, and prayers, you'll finish reading having a better grasp of our responsibility to be a love offering to Christ and to others.

—*Nicole Jacobsmeyer*
Speaker and author, *Take Back Your Joy*

Rachael beautifully illustrates God's desire for us to see, sense, and share His love. Her devotions offer opportunities for us to shift our focus off of ourselves and more toward loving others with intention, all while showing how God loves us deeply and completely. This book is one you'll be reaching for many times throughout your walk with Jesus—because we need the reminder of how loved we are and what it looks like to live sharing His love.

—*Chelsey DeMatteis*
Author, *More of Him, Less of Me*

In a world that is confused and boasts proudly, "Love is love," Rachael offers a glimpse into what true biblical love is. She incorporates Scripture with personal stories in this concise devotional that is easily applicable for any woman in any stage of life. It is only when we understand what God's love is and how to live it out that our life truly begins as a follower of Jesus Christ.

—*Tara Dew*
New Orleans Baptist Theological Seminary president's wife
Bible teacher and author, *Overflowing Joy*

Everyday Prayers for Love is perfect for the new believer or seasoned saint, inviting readers to go deeper into their faith in only a few minutes a day. Through transparency in her sharing of her own struggles, coupled with the timeless truths of Scripture, Rachael invites readers to experience Christ's compassion alongside the Holy Spirit's conviction. Each devotional is uplifting and engaging, but I especially enjoyed the opportunities for further study and personal reflection. I am grateful for the reminder of Christ's love for me and encouragement to show Jesus's love to others.

—*Laura R. Bailey*
Author and Bible teacher

In *Everyday Prayers for Love: Learning to Love God, Others, and Even Yourself,* Rachael crafts together daily practices for us to live out the love of God to others and ourselves. This devotional will guide you through Scripture to understand how God loves us and how we can show His love to others around us every day. It's a powerful and practical guide for our lives.

—*Natalia Drumm*
Bible teacher; creator, *Girlfriends in the Word*

Everyday Prayers for Love is a compelling and beautifully written guide that thoughtfully unpacks the true essence of love as defined by Scripture. With Jesus at the center, Rachael leads readers to a deeper understanding of what love is—and what it isn't—using 1 Corinthians 13 as her foundation. Each short devotional is paired with insightful reflection questions and prayers, making this book a must-have tool for anyone seeking to grow in love for God, others, and even themselves. I cannot recommend this book highly enough.

—*Jodie Niznik*
Host, *So Much More Scripture Meditation* podcast
Author, *Real People, Real Faith* Bible study series

Everyday Prayers for Love infused me with the essence of God's unconditional love and compelled me to live it out. One day at a time, hope and encouragement of God's goodness started to swell in and around me as Rachael's relatable personal stories and biblical examples solidified my belief in the blessed life portrayed in these pages. We can grow in a life of abundance as we steady our gaze on God's great love for us and the example He offered through the life of His Son, Jesus. This devotional will not only nurture your soul but will help set your eyes on the gift of God's perfect love, allow you the gift of loving others and Him back, and offer richer tastes of the continual blessings He delights to pour into your life.

—*Keri Eichberger*
Author, *Win over Worry*

Have you ever wondered what the definition of love truly is? Have you looked at the way the world is currently defining the word and known something was (majorly) off but felt helpless to do anything about it? Rachael Adams is here to be your guide. In this practical devotional, Rachael walks us through a biblical definition of love and helps us know not only how to love others in the world we live in today, but also how to function from a place of knowing *we* are deeply loved by God. It's just what the doctor ordered. Give yourself the gift of *Everyday Prayers for Love.*

—*Brooke McGlothlin*
Author and founder, Million Praying Moms
Host, *Everyday Prayers with Million Praying Moms* podcast

EVERYDAY
PRAYERS
— FOR —
LOVE

Learning to Love God, Others, and Even Yourself

RACHAEL ADAMS

WHITAKER
HOUSE

EVERYDAY PRAYERS FOR LOVE
Learning to Love God, Others, and Even Yourself

rachaelkadams.com
www.facebook.com/rachaeladamsauthor
www.instagram.com/rachaeladamsauthor

ISBN: 979-8-88769-284-5
eBook ISBN: 979-8-88769-285-2
Printed in the United States of America
© 2024 by Rachael Adams

Whitaker House | 1030 Hunt Valley Circle | New Kensington, PA 15068
www.whitakerhouse.com

Library of Congress Cataloging-in-Publication Data
Names: Adams, Rachael, 1983- author.
Title: Everyday prayers for love : learning to love God, others, and even
   yourself / Rachael Adams.
Description: New Kensington, PA : Whitaker House, [2024] | Summary: "A
   devotional and reflective journal written especially for women that uses
   Scripture readings to pray to God, designed to help readers gain an
   understanding of biblical love, learn how to love themselves, and live
   out love daily through their actions toward others"— Provided by
   publisher.
Identifiers: LCCN 2024020309 (print) | LCCN 2024020310 (ebook) | ISBN
   9798887692845 | ISBN 9798887692852 (ebook)
Subjects: LCSH: Love—Religious aspects—Christianity. | Prayers. | BISAC:
   RELIGION / Christian Living / Devotional Journal | FAMILY &
   RELATIONSHIPS / Love & Romance
Classification: LCC BS2675.6.L6 A43 2024 (print) | LCC BS2675.6.L6
   (ebook) | DDC 242/.643—dc23/eng/20240531
LC record available at https://lccn.loc.gov/2024020309
LC ebook record available at https://lccn.loc.gov/2024020310

1 2 3 4 5 6 7 8 9 10 11 ᄂᄂ� 31 30 29 28 27 26 25 24

DEDICATION

Lord, thank You for the love offering You
provided for me.
May my life, in return, be a love offering to You.

CONTENTS

PART TWO: LIVING OUT LOVE

FOREWORD

No subject has been covered so extensively or emphatically as *love*. From classic works of literature to the great love chapter of 1 Corinthians 13 to silly retro love songs and even modern-day viral marriage proposals seen by millions on social media, love captures our attention. We love our children, our significant others, our friends, and more. And as believers, we also love God. But just how much do we really understand about this most prevalent emotion?

To discover what love is all about, we can confidently begin with God's account of the greatest love ever shown, displayed throughout the pages of Scripture. It is within this narrative that we see not only what love is, but how love behaves. Most of all, we discover that the truest, purest form of unconditional love is embodied in Jesus Christ, our Lord and Savior. His life was lived in love. His death showed the vast depths of it. And His actions while here in the flesh serve as a vivid example of how we are to authentically love others.

Look at how Jesus answered a tough question from a religious leader, and what His answer teaches us about why we are on earth and what we should be doing while here:

> *"Teacher, which is the greatest commandment in the Law?" Jesus replied: "'Love the Lord your God with all your heart and with all your soul and with all your mind.' This is the first and greatest commandment. And the second is like it: 'Love your neighbor as yourself.' All the Law and the Prophets hang on these two commandments."*
> —Matthew 22:36–40

Jesus asserts that the entire teaching of God—all the law and the prophets—hinge upon these commands, which can be summed up in this three-step life plan:

1. Love God.

2. Love others.

3. Finally, love yourself.

Why are we here? To love. What are we supposed to do? Again: love. Love God and everyone else.

At this moment, you hold in your hands a powerful and practical devotional that will take you through thirty-one days of *Learning to Love God, Others, and Even Yourself. Everyday Prayers for Love* takes a deep dive into what biblical love truly is. The truths unearthed and the principles revealed will inspire you to love lavishly, beginning first with God, then extending to others. It will position you to comprehend what it means biblically to love yourself. (Hint: It is not the "you are enough" narcissistic self-love we see so prevalently displayed in culture today.)

However, gaining an understanding of the topic of love is not where this valuable resource stops. You will also be equipped with concrete ideas for fiercely and fearlessly loving others—your family, friends, neighbors, and even those who fall into the category of "enemies."

Rachael Adams will become more than an author to you as you experience this book. She will become a trusted friend and gentle guide who has not only lived her message, but who also has loved deeply. She longs for you to be swept away by the love of God so that you, in turn, can love those souls He puts in your path.

Your prayer life and your relationships are about to grow stronger. Your understanding of love will increase. And your faith in—and affection for—God will never be the same.

—Karen Ehman

New York Times bestselling author, *The Love Your Life Project*

ACKNOWLEDGMENTS

I am forever indebted to the people who made this devotional a reality. A special thanks to the Blythe Daniel Agency for being the first to believe in me as a writer. Blythe, your wisdom and support are invaluable. I know you care about this message, and I know you care about me.

Thank you, Christine Whitaker and the Whitaker House Publishing team, for pursuing this project. I am grateful to be included in your list of authors. I am so appreciative of the expertise of Peg Fallon and the entire editing team who took my words and made them better. I am equally thankful for the marketing team who helped take this message farther than I ever dreamed possible.

Thank you, Brooke McGlothlin and the Million Praying Moms ministry, for the opportunity to collaborate. I have been positively impacted both professionally and personally through our partnership.

Thank you, Megan Conner, for brainstorming and fine-tuning every word you see on these pages. I'm so grateful for your encouragement as an editor and as a friend.

To my mastermind group, I owe you an extra dose of gratitude for championing me and cheering me on. Thank you for challenging me to be more like Jesus.

To my local church for being the foundation and grounding for my ministry: Being a part of the body of believers has transformed my life for the better.

To my *Love Offering* podcast guests, listeners, and social media friends, I'm thankful to be living out my faith alongside you. I believe every interaction with you has mattered.

To my Marco Polo and Voxer friends, even though we live far apart, I hold you very near and dear to my heart.

To my local family and friends, thank you for loving me for who I am and for believing in me before I believed in myself. I am blessed to live life alongside you.

To you, who picked up this book, I am humbled. I pray it helps you believe how beloved you are by God and to learn to love how He created you. May your life be a love offering back to Him.

And thanks be to God. None of this would be a reality without Him. I give Him all of the glory.

INTRODUCTION

Nearly a decade ago, I was sitting in a church pew one Sunday morning when a love offering envelope caught my eye. Typically, these envelopes are for monetary giving, but at that moment, I sensed the Lord whisper to my heart, "You are My love offering. I've given you My love. Now how are you going to give My love to those around you?" The affections of my Lord had overflowed in my heart, and I could no longer keep it to myself. I wanted others to experience Him as well. But how could I share this precious gift with those who might need it most?

I knew the greatest commandments are to love the Lord with all my heart, mind, soul, and strength and to love my neighbor as myself. (See Matthew 22:36–40.) However, knowing this and then actually living it out were two very different things.

Soon after this encounter with the Lord, I began asking my family and friends about whether they struggled to live out this command too. I discovered I was not alone in feeling this tension. In a conversation with a friend, she suggested I interview people to hear how they were living out their faith. So, with much fear and trembling, I downloaded a free podcasting app and began reaching out to guests.

As I write this, I am wrapping up season six. To date, I have had the honor of interviewing over three hundred men and women. I feel fortunate to glean from so many amazing people, and I consider it one of God's greatest gifts. I pray it is a gift and an encouragement to all who tune in each week.

When I started *The Love Offering* podcast, I had no idea I'd be asked to write this devotional on *Everyday Prayers for Love* with Million Praying Moms and Whitaker House Publishing. Now I can see how beautifully God was preparing my heart and ministry. The podcast and the devotional complement one another so well.

I believe in the power of love with all my heart. That's why I'm so thankful you've picked up this devotional. We first explore what biblical love is in part one, walking through 1 Corinthians 13:4–8, which states:

> *Love is patient, love is kind. It does not envy, it does not boast, it is not proud. It does not dishonor others, it is not self-seeking, it is not easily angered, it keeps no record of wrongs. Love does not delight in evil but rejoices with the truth. It always protects, always trusts, always hopes, always perseveres. Love never fails.*

In each of these descriptions of biblical love, I hope you see how God exemplifies each characteristic and how you can too. By the end of part one, I pray this verse becomes your heartbeat, the life source sustaining all your thoughts and actions toward the Lord and others.

Then, in part two, we consider how to live out love to apply the knowledge we've received. It's my desire that this devotional transforms your whole being, thus affecting the lives around you. First, to realize how much God adores you. Then, to share His love with others so they may come to know and realize His love too. We need prayer every day to help us in this pursuit. That's why I appreciate the concept of the Million Praying Moms devotional series.

In the beginning seasons of *The Love Offering* podcast, I used to ask the same question: "How can we be a love offering?" I was amazed at the various responses I would receive based on the experience and background of my guest. Today, I'd love to hear your answer. Imagine a love offering envelope in front of you. Think about the person God is leading you to love tangibly. It could be your husband, child, parent, friend, pastor, teacher, stranger, neighbor, or even yourself. Who or what needs your affection and devotion today? Who is God laying on your heart?

You are on my heart as I write this. This devotional is my love offering to God and to you. My prayer is that the Lord meets you in a personal way on every page and that you feel His love in a way that you never have before.

And I pray that you, being rooted and established in love, … grasp how wide and long and high and deep is the love of Christ, and … know this love that surpasses knowledge—that you may be filled to the measure of all the fullness of God.
—Ephesians 3:17–19

I pray this not just for your sake, but also so that you may extend this newfound love to others. After all, *"We love because he first loved us"* (1 John 4:19).

My love to you in Christ Jesus,

Rachael

Note: This devotional uses Million Praying Moms' "Think, Pray, Praise" method of daily prayer. If you are not familiar with this prayer practice, please visit: www.millionprayingmoms.com/the-think-pray-praise-method-of-daily-prayer

PART ONE

WHAT IS BIBLICAL LOVE?

DAY 1

GOD IS LOVE

Whoever does not love does not know God,
because God is love.
—1 John 4:8

What is love? A group of adults posed this question to children. A seven-year-old named Danny answered, "Love is when my mommy makes coffee for my daddy and she takes a sip before giving it to him, to make sure the taste is OK." Mary Ann, age four, said, "Love is when your puppy licks your face even after you left him alone all day." Bobby, age seven, said love "is what's in the room with you at Christmas if you stop opening presents and listen."[1] Out of the mouth of babes, right?

Our current generation is inundated with books, songs, television shows, and movies that have all tried to explain love. However, their descriptions always seem to come up short. Scholars, poets, and screenwriters have attempted to contemplate the meaning of adoration—also to no avail. While humans have debated the true meaning of love for centuries, Scripture gives us the uncomplicated, pure definition: *"God is love"* (1 John 4:8).

Unfortunately, love has become a confusing term with little meaning. In most instances in our English language, we use the word *love* to describe our emotions about everything from food to family

---

1. Ladan Lashkari, "What Does Love Mean? See How 4-8 Year-Old Kids Describe Love," Daily Good, December 29, 2010, www.dailygood.org/story/158/what-does-love-mean-see-how-4-8-year-old-kids-describe-love-ladan-lashkari.

to God. However, biblical Greek has four different words to distinguish the various meanings of love: *eros* (romantic); *philia* (brotherly); *storge* (familiar); and *agape* (sacrificial). The authors use the Greek term *agape* in 1 John 4 and 1 Corinthians 13. Agape is a divine love that comes from God. It is superior to all other loves because it is the greatest and highest form, perfect, holy, and pure. Because God is eternal, His affection toward us will last forever. He is the origin *and* the culmination of love, the alpha and the omega.

SOMETHING TO THINK ABOUT

The apostle John asserts, *"Beloved, let us love one another, for love is from God, and whoever loves has been born of God and knows God"* (1 John 4:7 ESV). From this verse, we can conclude that God is the Source, the beginning of all things—mostly notably, the origin of love.

This truth is affirmed at the very beginning of the Bible: *"In the beginning God created the heavens and the earth"* (Genesis 1:1). He did not need to form the universe, yet God chose to make it. Why? Because adoration is best expressed toward something or someone else. God brought the world and humanity into existence as an expression of His own heart.

Throughout God's Word, it is evident that everything the Lord has done is motivated by love. His devotion has always involved choice and action. From Him, we learn that love isn't just a feeling; it is a verb. It is something we give, something we do. The apostle Paul provides us with a beautiful example of love in action in 1 Corinthians 13. He concludes his proclamation about love with the statement: *"And now these three remain: faith, hope and love. But the greatest of these is love"* (1 Corinthians 13:13).

We may have heard verses from this chapter read at many wedding ceremonies (they were read at mine!) but living out the characteristics can sometimes be difficult. Our human nature consistently fails to portray these attributes. Apart from the Holy Spirit, we cannot love like He does. God created us *"in his own image"* (Genesis 1:27). This gives us hope. If God is love, we can be too.

No matter what our various experiences and backgrounds are, when asked what love is, I hope we can all confidently answer: God is love, and He loves us. It's as simple as that.

EXTRA VERSES FOR STUDY OR PRAYER

1 Corinthians 13; 1 John 4

VERSE OF THE DAY

Whoever does not love does not know God, because God is love.
—1 John 4:8

PRAYER

Father, love can be so confusing. The world has tainted the term. Help me to understand You are the origin of love and how much You adore me. Let this be the foundation of all I think, say, and do. In Jesus's name, amen.

THINK

PRAY

PRAISE

_____

_____

_____

TO-DO   PRAYER LIST

_____   _____

_____   _____

_____   _____

QUESTIONS FOR DEEPER REFLECTION

1. How would you describe love? Do you typically view love as a feeling? When you view love as a verb, does that change your perspective?

_____

_____

_____

2. Does knowing the origin of love change the way you view God?

_____

_____

_____

DAY 2

LOVE IS PATIENT

The Lord is not slow in keeping his promise,
as some understand slowness. Instead he is patient with you,
not wanting anyone to perish,
but everyone to come to repentance.
—2 Peter 3:9

Nearly three decades later, I can still remember the "Heaven's Gates and Hell's Flames" play I attended at church. The flickering lights, eerie music, and impassioned actors created a vivid representation of the vast difference between the two eternal realities of heaven and hell. Watching from the pew, fear swept over me and brought me to my knees. With my head bowed and tears stinging my eyes, I prayed for God to save me. Coming to know God as my Savior was the beginning of my journey of faith.

Fast forward to my first job out of college. A woman was training me to be a community liaison for our state government. Though I didn't realize it initially, I received much more than training for my new job. She became the mentor I didn't know I needed by living out her faith in front of me. For the first time, I realized the possibility that God could be personal to me and affect my life now, not just in eternity.

Years passed, and I became a mother. Something about the responsibility of being a parent caused a sense of urgency in my heart. I began to read my Bible, pray, and get involved in church. The more time I spent with God, the more I learned of His love. I shifted from seeking Him to avoid hell to wanting to be with Him in heaven so I could experience His love eternally. I began to see Him as Father and myself as His beloved daughter.

For years, I selfishly fed myself spiritually until I realized I couldn't keep God's love all to myself. I began serving and sharing Him with others—just like my mentor had once done for me. I gave Him full access to my heart and my life, desiring to live for Him alone. Slowly, as I learned to surrender to His will, He became not just my Savior and Father but also my Lord.

As I reflect on my journey of faith, it amazes me that my relationship with Him continues to develop. I am now starting to recognize Him as my favorite person to talk to and be with. I'm beginning to know Him as my friend. While this is my unique journey, He desires a personal relationship with you too. Isn't it remarkable that the God of the universe wants to make Himself known to us? It is a joy and privilege to experience the depth of our Creator. What a gentleman He is to patiently reveal each loving layer of Himself as we become ready.

SOMETHING TO THINK ABOUT

Throughout the Scriptures, we witness God's patience for us by giving us time to quit living our way and begin living His way. One of my favorite examples of His forbearance is found in Luke 15:11–32, the parable of the lost or prodigal son. In the story, a man had two sons, the youngest of whom squandered all of his wealth through wild living. He ended up starving, finally came to his senses, and decided to return home. The father was filled with compassion when he spotted his son some distance away. He ran to his son, threw his arms around him, and kissed him. He brought out the best robe, a ring for his finger, and sandals for his son's feet. The father orchestrated a feast to celebrate because his son was lost and now was found.

This story is a tangible illustration of our relationship with our heavenly Father. He is patiently waiting for us too. No matter what we have done, He is looking toward the horizon, ready for us to come to our senses. He feels no condemnation, only compassion; He is ready to celebrate His child who was once lost and is now found. He longs to run to you with arms open wide.

God will search for us and give us opportunities to respond. He will not force us to come to Him, but once we do, He welcomes us into His loving embrace. He is patient with us, *"not wanting anyone to perish, but everyone to come to repentance"* (2 Peter 3:9). The father in the parable in Luke 15 forgave because he was filled with affection for his child. The challenge for us is to imitate the behavior of this father with the people in our lives. Just as God has exemplified long-suffering with us, we should be patient with others and even ourselves.

EXTRA VERSES FOR STUDY OR PRAYER
Galatians 5:22; Ephesians 4:2

VERSE OF THE DAY

The Lord is not slow in keeping his promise, as some understand slowness. Instead he is patient with you, not wanting anyone to perish, but everyone to come to repentance.   —2 Peter 3:9

PRAYER

Father, I'm grateful for Your patience with me. You have always pursued me and waited for me to come to You. Thank You for welcoming me with open arms. May I be patient with myself and not rush the process of sanctification. Help me to extend the same forbearance to the people in my life. In Jesus's name, amen.

THINK

PRAY

_____
_____
_____

PRAISE

_____
_____
_____

TO-DO   PRAYER LIST

_____   _____
_____   _____

QUESTIONS FOR DEEPER REFLECTION

1. Reflect on God's forbearance with you throughout your testimony. How has He been patient with you as you've navigated life apart from Him and alongside Him?

_____
_____

2. Would you consider yourself a patient person? Do you typically get frustrated with yourself, others, and even God? How can you better embody this fruit of the Spirit?

_____
_____

DAY 3

LOVE IS KIND

Therefore, as God's chosen people, holy and dearly loved,
clothe yourselves with compassion, kindness, humility,
gentleness and patience.
—Colossians 3:12

You're going to need a full hysterectomy."

My doctor delivered this statement over the phone, the day before Thanksgiving. Before we hung up, she also shared that my recent blood test results were concerning, and she was referring me to a surgical oncologist. While I was not thankful for this news, my heart still understood the need for gratitude, especially in light of the upcoming holiday.

As I told my friends and family about my prognosis, they interceded on my behalf. They prayed for my healing, for me to feel God's presence, and for my mind to be at peace in the days leading up to the operation.

Their prayers worked. From the moment I opened my eyes the morning of my surgery until the nurses wheeled me into the operating room, I felt a peace that *"surpasses all understanding"* (Philippians 4:7 ESV). I had prayed for rescue and mercy. God answered my requests through His presence. His intervention came in the form of His Spirit, and it was manifested through my loved ones, doctors, and nurses.

Later, when I recounted my health journey to a friend, I had an epiphany. I told her, "Never had I been in such pain, but never had I felt more loved." What a strange tension this was, but one I was oddly grateful for.

During this experience, I was showered with prayers, emails, texts, calls, social media messages, cards, and gifts. My loved ones' gestures truly brought me joy in the midst of my sorrow. Their acts of benevolence helped me realize that God's kindness is not only offered by our heavenly Father to His children, but is often displayed through His people.

The outpouring of generosity continued well after my surgery and sparked a new appreciation for the beautiful community God had given me. It reminded me what a difference our service to others through word, prayer, presence, gift, or deed can make. Even on the occasions when I was unkind to myself, the people in my life displayed tangible reminders of God's affection for me and eased the pain of my recovery. Knowing the difference their love offerings made challenges me to do the same for others who are struggling.

I'm beyond grateful that my biopsy results were benign, but I also want to be sensitive to the fact that you might not have received the desired answer to your prayer or weren't surrounded by such a generous community. If that is the case, my heart hurts for you. As my experience shows, God's intervention may result in your healing, but it might not. Regardless of the outcome, His divine provision always comes in the form of His presence and peace amid your trials. And as illustrated earlier, His involvement is often displayed through His people. Could His kindness also be expressed through you?

SOMETHING TO THINK ABOUT

God exhibits this everlasting, compassionate amiability toward us (see Isaiah 54:8), and we are responsible for continuing His example within our relationships. While we know we must be *"kind and compassionate to one another"* (Ephesians 4:32), sometimes that's easier said than done. Showing kindheartedness doesn't always come naturally. It takes practice. Through Him, we can exhibit this fruit of the Spirit because His power *"is at work within us"* (Ephesians 3:20).

A beautiful example of compassion is illustrated in 1 Samuel through the relationship between Jonathan and David. Their friendship is one of the deepest and closest recorded in the Bible. Jonathan was the prince of Israel and should have been the next king, but God chose David instead. However, this did not diminish Jonathan's love for David.

Jonathan's father, Saul, became envious as people became devoted to David. In a jealous rage, Saul attempted to murder David, forcing Jonathan to deal with conflicting allegiances to his father, the king, and his best friend. Regardless of the consequences, Jonathan decided to alert David of Saul's diabolical plan, and as a result, David's life was spared.

Years later, because of their sworn friendship, David took great pains to invite Jonathan's son, Mephibosheth, into his palace to live. (See 2 Samuel 9.) David was generous, partly because of his loyalty to God's previously anointed king but mainly because he vowed to show benevolence to Jonathan's descendants.

Jonathan and David's friendship was based on their commitment to God, not just each other. They allowed nothing to come between them. Their relationship grew closer through every test, and their friendship endured until death parted them.

EXTRA VERSES FOR STUDY OR PRAYER
Ephesians 4:32; 1 Peter 3:8

VERSE OF THE DAY

Therefore, as God's chosen people, holy and dearly loved, clothe yourselves with compassion, kindness, humility, gentleness and patience.   —Colossians 3:12

PRAYER

Father, thank You for Your kindness. I'm grateful You don't expect me to repay it. How could I? Help me to recognize the kindness of others toward me and not take it for granted. Prompt me to be sensitive to the needs of those around me, and through Your Spirit, enable me to be kind. In Jesus's name, amen.

THINK

PRAY

PRAISE

TO-DO

PRAYER LIST

QUESTIONS FOR DEEPER REFLECTION

1. Who has been kind to you recently? Who has been unkind to you? What steps, if any, do you feel the Lord calling you to take toward those people?

2. How has the Lord been compassionate toward you? How can you clothe yourself with kindness and extend generosity toward those around you?

_____

_____

_____

DAY 4

LOVE DOES NOT ENVY

A heart at peace gives life to the body, but envy rots the bones.
—Proverbs 14:30

I had never attended a writers' conference before. After obtaining my agenda and name tag that first morning of the convention, I tried to navigate through a sea of over six hundred women with a dream similar to mine—to publish a book. Unsure of my surroundings or who to talk to, I found a seat alone to gather my thoughts.

As I looked around the room, my confidence waned. I saw women talking easily, laughing, exchanging business cards, and hugging as if they already knew each other. Adding to my discomfort, the women were absolutely stunning. While I should have celebrated the beauty of God's creation before me, I judged my projected imperfections against them, which only caused my insecurities to increase.

As I continued to scan the room, the agent I wanted to sign with caught my eye. Weeks before, I had stalked the conference guide so I would recognize the faces of the agents and editors in case I ran into them throughout the weekend. The agent had a group of women around her. They were likely her clients because it was evident they all knew each other well. I watched them interact—not knowing who they were but wanting what they had.

God didn't grant me "what they had" that weekend. The desired divine appointment with the agent did not come into fruition. But I was able to meet so many incredible sisters in Christ, and God was preparing my heart in a plethora of other ways. Clearly, there was work to be done on my sanctification.

Fast forward a year later, when I returned to the same conference. This time, I wasn't so green in experience or envy. I was more comfortable in my own skin and recognized some familiar faces. I was able to laugh, talk, and hug friends I'd kept in touch with from the previous year. Fortunately, I was granted a meeting with the agent I desired, and the hoped-for connection was made. However, I could empathize with the woman in the background who, like me just one year prior, sat watching alone from her seat.

Although God saw fit to grant me the desire of my heart, as evidenced by the book you hold in your hands, if I'm being gut-level honest, I still struggle with comparison. Even as a Christian author, I see women achieving what I wish I could. And while I am happy for them, a tinge of jealousy emerges. *Why not me?* The green-eyed monster still shows up more often than I care to admit.

SOMETHING TO THINK ABOUT

What about you? Is there a person or group of people you wish your life could mimic?

When someone succeeds or accomplishes something we wish we could do, it is difficult not to be envious of them, isn't it? We may celebrate them to their faces, but we are often jealous beneath our joyful facade.

Knowing we would struggle in this area, God added a clear directive in the Ten Commandments. He said, "*You shall not covet your neighbor's house. You shall not covet your neighbor's wife, or his male or female servant, his ox or donkey, or anything that belongs to your neighbor*" (Exodus 20:17). In other words, we shouldn't resent others who have what we may think we lack.

To stop or prevent covetous behavior, we must practice being content with what God has given us and celebrate what God has given to others. Another person's success and calling do not threaten ours. God has uniquely created each individual with certain talents and abilities.

Instead of envying what they have, we should cheer for our brothers and sisters in Christ and be grateful for our own unique giftings. After all, don't we long for people to rejoice with us when it is our turn to succeed?

Through this lens, we should see one another as co-laborers and collaborators as opposed to competitors. When we learn to be content with who we are, we are no longer pining for someone else's life because we trust in God's sovereignty for the assignments He's given us. Love compels us to root for each other as we strive toward our dreams. If not, our hearts will always be aching for something missing, a longing only God can fill. Look to Him for your contentment, and you will find there is nowhere else you'd rather be than in His presence. With Him, there is nothing else you need.

EXTRA VERSES FOR STUDY OR PRAYER

Exodus 20:17; Proverbs 23:17

VERSE OF THE DAY

A heart at peace gives life to the body, but envy rots the bones.
—Proverbs 14:30

PRAYER

Lord, thank You for how You've created me and for the unique blessings and gifts You have given me. Forgive me for being covetous of others' personalities, appearance, possessions, and accomplishments. When I start feeling envious of another person, remind me to celebrate with them and genuinely desire their success. Help me not to be complacent but to be content with myself. In Jesus's name, amen.

THINK

PRAY

_____

_____

_____

PRAISE

_____

_____

_____

TO-DO   **PRAYER LIST**

_____   _____

_____   _____

_____   _____

QUESTIONS FOR DEEPER REFLECTION

1. Who do you envy? What do you feel they have but you lack? What environment usually triggers this emotion in you most?

_____

_____

2. When you hear someone sharing good news, do you react with celebration rather than jealousy? How can you intentionally cheer for others instead of viewing them as competitors?

_____

_____

_____

DAY 5

LOVE DOES NOT BOAST

Therefore, as it is written:
"Let the one who boasts boast in the Lord."
—1 Corinthians 1:31

There was a college-aged girl whose voice I loved to hear as she led worship on Sundays. She was a summer intern, and I had the opportunity to meet her family one morning after service. As I celebrated their daughter's God-given talent, her parents' eyes lit up with delight.

"What makes your daughter so unique is that she doesn't realize how special she is. Or at least she doesn't let on that she does!" I continued in praise of her vocal ability and humble posture. Of all the times I'd heard her sing, I never had the impression that she gloated in the giftings the Lord has given her—which makes her talent all the more beautiful for everyone in the congregation to receive!

Her dad agreed with me wholeheartedly, bursting with pride as he told me more stories about his daughter. The college-aged worship leader blushed in embarrassment and asked her dad to quit exulting her. He smiled and obliged, declaring that praising her was one of his favorite pastimes. As a fellow parent, I understood his sentiment. I'm the same way with my children. I don't know how often I catch myself saying, "Not to brag, but let me tell you what Will and Kate did/said ..."

During my conversation that Sunday, it occurred to me that our heavenly Father likely feels the same way about us as His children. Imagine Him saying, "Let Me tell you what *(insert your name)* did today. I'm so proud of how she used the abilities I gave her without expecting any accolades or glory for herself. There was no hint of self-importance or need to be seen."

Have you ever considered that God looks upon us as His daughters and when we use the talents He has given us, He rejoices over us with singing? (See Zephaniah 3:17.) He longs to commend us like any other proud parent would. Don't you love the thought of that?

SOMETHING TO THINK ABOUT

If there is anyone in the Bible who could laud his accomplishments, it's Paul. I imagine people admired him during his lifetime, and it would have been tempting to draw attention to himself. But because of his love for Christ, he focused his testimony on all God had done in his life. Paul testified:

Whatever anyone else dares to boast about—I am speaking as a fool—I also dare to boast about. Are they Hebrews? So am I. Are they Israelites? So am I. Are they Abraham's descendants? So am I. Are they servants of Christ? (I am out of my mind to talk like this.) I am more. I have worked much harder, been in prison more frequently, been flogged more severely, and been exposed to death again and again. Five times I received from the Jews the forty lashes minus one. Three times I was beaten with rods, once I was pelted with stones, three times I was shipwrecked, I spent a night and a day in the open sea, I have been constantly on the move. I have been in danger from rivers, in danger from bandits, in danger from my fellow Jews, in danger from Gentiles; in danger in the city, in danger in the country, in danger at sea; and in danger from false believers. I have labored and toiled and have often gone without sleep; I have known hunger and thirst and have often gone without food; I have been cold and naked. Besides everything else, I face daily the pressure of my concern for all the churches. Who is weak, and I do not feel weak? Who is led into sin, and I do not inwardly burn? If I must boast, I will boast of the things that show my weakness.

—2 Corinthians 11:21–30

In addition to this discourse, Paul called all he accomplished "*rubbish*" compared to the greatness "*of knowing Christ*" (Philippians 3:8 ESV). Paul did not depend on deeds to please God or confirm his own value. Neither should we, because the most impressive human credentials will always fall short of God's holy standards.

Even when Jesus lived among us, He never magnified His miraculous works and good deeds. Instead, He proclaimed, "*By myself I can do nothing*" (John 5:30). His motive was to please His Father and to glorify the One who sent Him. This, too, should be our goal as we express our love to others through our actions, talents, and resources. May we give credit where credit is due. The next time we are tempted to brag, may our love for the Lord lead us to boast of His great name. He alone is worthy of our praise.

EXTRA VERSES FOR STUDY OR PRAYER
Jeremiah 9:24; Luke 18:14

VERSE OF THE DAY

Therefore, as it is written: "Let the one who boasts boast in the Lord."
—1 Corinthians 1:31

PRAYER

Father, thank You for all You have given to me. Forgive me for taking credit or trying to gain glory for what You alone deserve. Cleanse my heart from any impure motive or thought that causes me to extol myself and seek man's applause. If I boast, may it be of the ways You have blessed me and worked in my life. I pray if I make much of anything, I make much of You. May my desire be to make Your name known and exalted. In Jesus's name, amen.

THINK

_____

_____

_____

PRAY

_____

_____

_____

PRAISE

_____

_____

_____

TO-DO

_____

_____

_____

PRAYER LIST

_____

_____

_____

QUESTIONS FOR DEEPER REFLECTION

1. How do others make you feel when they draw attention to their achievements and accolades? In what ways have you been singing your own praises? Do you think you do this to receive the applause of man?

_____

_____

_____

2. How can you intentionally boast about God and others? Make a list of the things you can exult about in the Lord.

_____

_____

_____

DAY 6

LOVE IS NOT PROUD

For everyone who exalts himself will be humbled, but the one who humbles himself will be exalted.
—Luke 18:14 (ESV)

Do you need help?" an elderly gentleman asked as I struggled to grab groceries from my car. I had recently started volunteering with Project 58:10, a feeding program inspired by Isaiah 58:10 that provides prepacked meals for hungry children in my community. The nonprofit began when a bystander witnessed a child eating paper one Friday afternoon at school, trying to fill her stomach before the weekend. These families humble themselves and graciously accept aid from complete strangers, something I tend to struggle to do myself.

I first began volunteering with Project 58:10 when Will was a toddler and Kate was a baby. I would pick up the grocery shipment and then deliver it to the church. Attempting to deliver cases of food with a baby and toddler in tow proved to be challenging, to say the least. I had Kate secured to my chest with a cloth wrap and held Will's hand so he wouldn't venture into the street. With my one free hand, I carried the grocery shipment.

So when this stranger approached me and asked if I needed help, my first reaction was to refuse his offer. *I could carry these heavy loads with two kids attached!* (*Insert eye roll.*) It might take me twice as long, but I was determined to do this job all on my own. But when I saw the kindness in the man's eyes, I laid down my stubborn pride and accepted his helping hand.

This man saw a woman in distress and reacted with generosity. Unloading my bags was a simple gesture at the time. Subsequently, he began serving regularly in the Project 58:10 ministry and delivering the bags to schools and children's homes in the summer. Spending so much time together tending to the needs of others forged a treasured bond between us and resulted in the unexpected blessing of another grandfather figure, whom we now know as Jim, enriching the lives of my family. I often think about what would have happened if I had let my ego win and refused his assistance.

SOMETHING TO THINK ABOUT

Pride tops the list of sins God hates; Proverbs 6:17 refers to it as *"haughty eyes."* Pride can mean a feeling of superiority or exaggerated self-esteem. Not only does the Bible say, *"God opposes the proud"* (James 4:6), but it warns, *"Pride goes before destruction, a haughty spirit before a fall"* (Proverbs 16:18).

The opposite of our ego-driven failings is humility. John the Baptist epitomized a humble spirit. To contextualize his story, we must remember that Israel had not seen a prophet for more than four hundred years. People were eagerly awaiting the Messiah, so when John began prophesying, many confused him for the long-awaited Savior. He spoke with authority, causing multitudes to respond to his message of repentance. However, even as crowds were drawn to him, he pointed beyond himself, never forgetting that his main role was to announce the arrival of Jesus.

Although John was well-known, he was content for Jesus to take the higher place. When the people questioned who he was, John responded that he was not even worthy to be Christ's slave, to perform the humble task of unfastening his shoes. (See John 1:27.) Yet Jesus said John was the greatest of all the prophets. (See Luke 7:26–28.) If an individual of such renown felt inadequate to even be Christ's slave, how much more should we lay aside our prideful nature?

Our conceit vanishes when we realize who Jesus is. He came as a servant and taught, *"For all those who exalt themselves will be humbled, and those who humble themselves will be exalted"* (Luke 18:14). Our self-importance melts away when we truly understand the character of Christ. May we have the posture of John the Baptist so that we can love others as he and Jesus exemplified through their servanthood.

EXTRA VERSES FOR STUDY OR PRAYER
Luke 7:28; 2 Timothy 3:1–5

VERSE OF THE DAY

For everyone who exalts himself will be humbled, but the one who humbles himself will be exalted.　　—Luke 18:14 (ESV)

PRAYER

Lord, change the posture of my heart. Reinforce that my purpose is to point people to You. Forgive me for behaving pridefully. I know You oppose the proud and show favor to the humble. Help me be content to let You take the higher place. May I accept help willingly and offer aid generously. In Jesus's name, amen.

THINK

_____

_____

_____

PRAY

_____

_____

_____

PRAISE

_____

_____

_____

TO-DO   ## PRAYER LIST

_____   _____

_____   _____

_____   _____

QUESTIONS FOR DEEPER REFLECTION

1. Do you accept help easily? Why or why not? How can you display God's love by humbling yourself to accept assistance from others and offer to provide aid for those in need?

_____

_____

2. Do you struggle with pride? In what areas might God be asking you to humble yourself?

_____

_____

DAY 7

LOVE DOES NOT DISHONOR OTHERS

Be devoted to one another in love.
Honor one another above yourselves.
—Romans 12:10

I still remember where I was sitting on the couch that day. I was nestled in the middle of my two brothers when my mom and dad told us they were getting a divorce. I was eight years old and in second grade. It was evident their marriage was over before they spoke the words. However, once they told us, that made it official. Life as I knew it, as a family of five, had ended.

Decisions like divorce are difficult for everyone involved. Honestly, even thirty years later, their choice still occasionally triggers old wounds. And as challenging as this circumstance has been, and likely will continue to be, the older I get, the more compassion I have for my mom and dad. I recently read a quote on social media that said, "Be patient with your parents. This is their first time living too."

Reflecting on my relationships with my mother and father, I know they love me. They have always been there for me, sacrificed on my behalf, and made an effort to show they care. They have done their best, and their intentions have always been for my good.

Of course, I wish things would have turned out differently, but I am thankful for the parents God designed for me. While their choice has become part of my story, I can decide how I respond to the cards I've been dealt. Regardless of the outcome, I've resolved to honor them. They are good people with beautiful hearts. I refuse to dishonor them based on the paths they have taken. Instead, I can honestly say I respect them and admire their resilience, courage, and strength.

Now that I'm a parent, I better understand how tough marriage and parenting can be. Despite my best efforts, it wouldn't shock me if someday, my children need to process some of the things I've unknowingly burdened their hearts with. However, I pray they will choose to have compassion and honor me as their mom. Like my parents before me, this too is my first time living.

SOMETHING TO THINK ABOUT

God created mankind with dignity and honor. However, by the time Jesus was born, women had lost their honorable standing in society. During the intertestamental period—the four hundred years between the prophet Malachi and John the Baptist—women were no longer viewed with respect. Instead, they were degraded to a place of shame. This was largely due to a group of pious Jewish men who stood up against the invasion of Hellenism to an extreme. In fact, one highly regarded Jewish leader named Ben Sira taught that women were the source of sin.[2]

Throughout Jesus's life, we witness Him removing women's shame and restoring their honor.[3] He did not treat women as others in His culture did.

Consider the adulterous woman whom the religious leaders wanted to stone to death. Jesus said, *"Let him who is without sin among you be the first to throw a stone at her"* (John 8:7 ESV). Because He was without sin, Jesus could have thrown the stone if He chose to do so. However, He told the woman He would not condemn her. Jesus saved her from their wrath and restored her dignity.

2. Alice Ogden Bellis, "Eve: Apocrypha," *Shalvi/Hyman Encyclopedia of Jewish Women,* Jewish Women's Archive, March 20, 2009, jwa.org/encyclopedia/article/eve-apocrypha.
3. Kristi McLelland, *Jesus and Women: In the First Century and Now* (Nashville, TN: Lifeway Press, 2022).

As Christians, we should not be casting stones in judgment either. We should never dishonor, degrade, or shame others no matter what they have done. As Jesus demonstrated during His life on earth, we should highly regard one another, recognizing we are all created in God's image and all fall short of His glory. This kind of regard goes far beyond pretense and politeness. I pray our consideration of others indicates our reverence and honor for those God has placed in our lives, most specifically our Lord, Jesus, who we aim to esteem above all.

EXTRA VERSES FOR STUDY OR PRAYER

Exodus 20:12; Ephesians 6:1–3

VERSE OF THE DAY

Be devoted to one another in love. Honor one another above yourselves.   —Romans 12:10

PRAYER

Father, forgive me when I degrade others. It is not my place to cast stones. Help me to absolve those who have shamed me. I don't want to live in disgrace or regret. Free me from these feelings. Thank You for showing me how to respect and honor people regardless of their behavior and decisions. I know I fall short of Your glory every single day, yet You continue to love me. May I never forget the magnitude of that. In Jesus's name, amen.

THINK

PRAY

_____

_____

_____

PRAISE

_____

_____

_____

TO-DO

_____

_____

_____

PRAYER LIST

_____

_____

_____

QUESTIONS FOR DEEPER REFLECTION

1. What are you doing to show respect to your parents? Are you living in a way that brings honor to them?

    _____

    _____

2. When was the last time you felt honored by someone? When you felt dishonored? Who is one person in your immediate circle you can proactively esteem today?

    _____

    _____

DAY 8

LOVE IS NOT SELF-SEEKING

And when you pray, do not be like the hypocrites, for they love to pray standing in the synagogues and on the street corners to be seen by others. Truly I tell you, they have received their reward in full.
—Matthew 6:5

Every day at noon for one month, our pastor organized various leaders in our church to facilitate a different topic of prayer for our community. My pastor asked if I would lead one of the gatherings. Although I was nervous to speak in front of a large congregation, I accepted the invitation.

I spent hours studying in preparation for the prayer meeting. I dressed in my Sunday finest on a Tuesday and arrived at 11:30 a.m. to ensure I got myself situated. I sat in the first pew with my highlighted outline and leatherbound Bible. Fidgeting, I glanced from my notes to my watch and then back again to my notes.

At 11:55, I found it odd that no one had entered the sanctuary yet. I assured myself they were probably rushing from work or grabbing a quick lunch. As the clock struck noon, I started to second-guess myself. *Did I have the right location?* I double-checked my calendar. I triple-checked my texts. Yes, I was in the right place at the right time. Yet I was alone. No one showed up for the service but me.

At first, I was aggravated. I thought, "You've got to be kidding. I spent hours preparing for a message I won't deliver, and prayers no one will hear." And then, the sting of conviction pricked my heart. Maybe the message was for me and me alone. I tucked my papers back into my Bible, rose from the pew, and sank to my knees at the altar.

In a sanctuary built for a thousand, I knelt alone before God's throne. Not because I was so holy but because I realized how far from holy I was. God cleared my schedule and everyone else's (it seemed) to provide space to experience communion with Him. I may have been selfishly desiring something else that day when, all the while, He'd simply been seeking time with me.

After all, only five people attended the day before. Why did I think the church would be filled with people who wanted to hear from *me?* Maybe God did instead.

SOMETHING TO THINK ABOUT

Prior to this experience, I never would have thought the following Scripture would be applicable in my life. However, I'm guilty of what Jesus told His disciples not to do. In Matthew 6, He says:

And when you pray, do not be like the hypocrites, for they love to pray standing in the synagogues and on the street corners to be seen by others. Truly I tell you, they have received their reward in full. But when you pray, go into your room, close the door and pray to your Father, who is unseen. Then your Father, who sees what is done in secret, will reward you. —Matthew 6:5–6

I want to be clear; this isn't a slight against public prayer. There is certainly a time and a place for that. In fact, the gospel records Jesus praying both privately and publicly. (See, for example, Matthew 14:23 and 14:19, respectively.) The point isn't where we communicate with God, but the posture of our hearts when we do.

So how do we move from hypocritical to heartfelt? What does authentic and submissive prayer look like? Thankfully, Jesus doesn't just leave us with instructions on how *not* to pray; He gives us a guide in what we now call the Lord's Prayer:

Our Father in heaven, hallowed be your name, your kingdom come, your will be done, on earth as it is in heaven. Give us today

our daily bread. And forgive us our debts, as we also have for-
given our debtors. And lead us not into temptation, but deliver
us from the evil one.   —Matthew 6:9–13

Through this prayer, Jesus models how we should approach our heavenly Father. Above all, we should honor the holiness and deity of God. We worship Him first for who He is, then we beseech God for His perfect purposes to be accomplished in this world and the next. Keeping these objectives at the forefront of our thoughts guards us against becoming self-seeking. Instead of desiring our name, our kingdom, and our will first, our greatest longing is pursuing His name, His kingdom, and His purposes. He is *always* our greatest reward.

EXTRA VERSES FOR STUDY OR PRAYER
Matthew 6:9–13; Luke 11:2–4

VERSE OF THE DAY

And when you pray, do not be like the hypocrites, for they love to
pray standing in the synagogues and on the street corners to be
seen by others. Truly I tell you, they have received their reward in
full.   —Matthew 6:5

PRAYER

Father, thank You for being willing to communicate with me and being available to listen. Forgive me for acting in ways that were self-seeking to gain attention for myself. I don't want to be hypocritical. I want everything I say and do to be heartfelt, with a pure motive to honor Your name and bring You glory. Let Your kingdom come, and Your will be done. In Jesus's name, amen.

THINK

_____

_____

_____

PRAY

_____

_____

_____

PRAISE

_____

_____

_____

TO-DO

_____

_____

_____

PRAYER LIST

_____

_____

_____

QUESTIONS FOR DEEPER REFLECTION

1. Have you ever experienced a time you realized you had the wrong motives for serving God? If so, how did He redirect your focus to seek Him first in your service?

_____

_____

2. What steps do you need to take to devote more time for communion with the Lord? How can you consciously ensure you seek to glorify God's name, His kingdom, and His will instead of your own?

_____

_____

DAY 9

LOVE IS NOT
EASILY ANGERED

The Lord is gracious and merciful,
slow to anger and abounding in steadfast love.
—Psalm 145:8 (esv)

One of my absolute favorite pastimes is cheering for my kids at their extracurricular activities. Whether on a field, in a gym, in the pool, or on a stage, I can't wait to support them—you will just find me in a different seat each time.

I typically show up at these events in head-to-toe team apparel. I even bring my cowbell since my voice gets hoarse from hollering. I should note here that I am typically a very low-key person everywhere except at my children's extracurricular activities. I'm not sure what it is about these occasions that brings out my alter ego. I think it's because I want so badly for my children to be happy and watching them do what they love brings me such joy.

In one such instance, I sat beside my husband at a semi-state football championship game watching my son, Will. It was the fourth quarter, and the game was close. Tensions were high, to say the least. Will was playing quarterback, and he threw an incomplete pass. The entire crowd let out a disgusted sigh. My heart sank.

Then, a man behind me screamed, "That was a terrible throw!" This time, my heart skipped a beat. That was *my son* he was talking about. I turned around in rage to see who had made that comment, and to my surprise, it was a father from our own team! I stared at him until he noticed I had heard his comment about Will.

"I heard what you said!" I yelled back at him and turned around filled with loathing. Oh, my blood was boiling! Was it a bad throw? Yes. But would I let anyone talk about my son like that? No!

Luckily, Will completed many of his other passes, and we won the game. I was thrilled for his team, but I was frustrated I'd let my negative emotions get the better of me. Even though our team was victorious, I experienced a personal loss.

It wasn't the first time I'd let someone's comments about my kids cause my temper to flare. I may claim it's a mother's protective instinct to defend her children, but I also must guard my Christian witness carefully.

Everyone around me saw the interaction during that game and observed how I behaved, but they didn't see my apology to the man afterwards. I asked for his forgiveness for allowing my raw emotions to triumph. And while I only needed to make amends with God and that man, I would not have been in that situation in the first place had I kept my character in check. It's just a game, after all.

God has given us our feelings for a reason. Scripture clearly states anger in itself is not wrong. We simply must not sin when we are infuriated, as I did. (See Ephesians 4:26.)

SOMETHING TO THINK ABOUT

When you read the Gospels, Jesus's ministry is characterized by turning the other cheek. (See Matthew 5:38–40.) However, there are a few recorded occasions when even Jesus felt indignation at the actions and behavior of those around Him. We read about His frustration leading Him to curse the unfruitful fig tree and overturn the money changers' tables in the temple. (See, respectively, Mark 11:12–14, 15–17.) But since Jesus was without sin, we know there was no wrongdoing when we see these examples of His anger.

In another instance, Jesus was angry and *"deeply distressed"* about the Pharisees' uncaring response to a man with a shriveled hand on the Sabbath (Mark 3:5). Instead of directing His irritation toward them, He corrected the problem by healing the man's hand.

The Bible doesn't tell us that we shouldn't have ill feelings but rather that we should handle our exasperation properly. If vented thoughtlessly, outrage can hurt others and destroy relationships. If bottled up inside, it can cause us to become bitter and destroy us from within. Too often, we express our fury in selfish and harmful ways. In contrast, Jesus expressed His displeasure by correcting the problem.

Following the Lord's example, we should be *"quick to listen, slow to speak and slow to become angry, because human anger does not produce the righteousness that God desires"* (James 1:19–20). The next time you feel your temperature rise, consider how you can pour water on the flame rather than gas. As Proverbs 15:1 says, *"A gentle answer turns away wrath, but a harsh word stirs up anger."* I pray we confront our fury in a way that builds relationships rather than destroys them. And like Jesus, may we only use our righteous rage to uncover constructive solutions rather than destructive separations. Now that would be something to holler about!

EXTRA VERSES FOR STUDY OR PRAYER

Exodus 34:6; Ephesians 4:26

VERSE OF THE DAY

The Lord is gracious and merciful, slow to anger and abounding in steadfast love. —Psalm 145:8 (esv)

PRAYER

Father, thank You for being slow to anger when You have every reason to be irritated and aggravated with me. Forgive me for losing my temper so easily. If I get upset, may it be over an injustice where, through Your Holy Spirit, I can find a loving solution. May my emotions not destroy relationships but help all of us who aim to follow in Your footsteps to pursue righteousness at all times. In Jesus's name, amen.

THINK

_____
_____
_____

PRAY

_____
_____
_____

PRAISE

_____
_____
_____

TO-DO   PRAYER LIST

_____   _____
_____   _____
_____   _____

QUESTIONS FOR DEEPER REFLECTION

1. Are you angry with someone right now? What can you do to resolve your differences?

_____
_____

2. How would you define righteous anger versus unrighteous frustration? Do you think God would be pleased with what you are upset about and how you handle your aggravations?

_____

_____

_____

DAY 10

LOVE KEEPS NO RECORD
OF WRONGS

As high as the heavens are above the earth, so great is his love
for those who fear him; as far as the east is from the west,
so far has he removed our transgressions from us.
—Psalm 103:11–12

I surveyed the lamplit room of middle and high school-aged girls deep in thought. The glow made them look so beautiful, but I could see the hurt in their eyes even with the dim lighting. During this Night of Agape for preteen and teen girls, we'd laughed after I showed pictures of myself at their ages, especially the photographs with my barrel-rolled bangs and rollerblades. But the night took a more serious turn when I shared my testimony and some of the core beliefs I'd had about myself as a young woman. Those beliefs greatly affected choices I made and the consequences that stemmed from those decisions.

After delivering my story, I allowed the young ladies time for introspection. They were each given a blank canvas and tasked with drawing the outline of a cross. Inside the frame, I instructed them to note anything they metaphorically wanted to lay down on the cross. I offered them space to write out any dismal thoughts that came to their minds about themselves—decisions they regretted, mistakes they'd made, sins they'd committed, or feelings of inadequacy or worthlessness because of what others had said or done to them.

I was amazed at how full the crosses were on each of the five-by-seven-inch canvases that were blank just five minutes prior. Girls wrote steadily and without hesitation, pouring their feelings out to the Lord. As I walked around the room, glancing at their souls inscribed on the coarse cloth, my heart grieved as I noticed repetition and similarity in their pain and shame. But then, with even more vitality, my heart leapt with hope as I realized God already knew everything those girls had written. There were no surprises here. God still loved them despite it all.

To complete the activity, I gave each young woman a red marker. I asked them to cross out everything they had previously listed on the canvas, symbolizing God's agape love vanquishing the darkness of the past they had just laid down. There was something therapeutic about the exercise, seeing each transgression canceled with every red swipe until all they could see was Christ's blood erasing years of heartache.

SOMETHING TO THINK ABOUT

The teenage girls at this special event learned God does not keep a log of our trespasses. Isn't this unfathomable?! When God forgives our sin, He separates the offense from us and doesn't even remember it! (See Hebrews 8:12.) While we may have difficulty forgetting, the Lord absolves our failings as long as we confess and repent. And once we receive His merciful gift, we must pass it on to others. For we are told, *"Bear with each other and forgive one another if any of you has a grievance against someone. Forgive as the Lord forgave you"* (Colossians 3:13).

Remembering how much God has forgiven you is the key to extending the same grace to those who may have done you wrong. What would happen if we, too, removed the transgressions of others *"as far as the east is from the west"* (Psalm 103:12)? Instead of wallowing in offense and dredging up the past, what if we wiped everyone's slates clean? Are you keeping score today? I pray we no longer keep a record of wrongs and instead choose to forgive, forget, and reconcile with others as far as it is up to us.

This concept applies to our own account of sin—holding on to a ledger of our misconduct as well. If I were with you right now, I'd hand you a canvas and a red marker. And while it's true our canvases would likely be overflowing with failures, through true repentance, the blood of Jesus Christ erases our past, present, and future offenses. Allow this truth to wash over your heart today: No matter what you've done or what's been done to you, *"Though your sins are like scarlet, they shall be as white as snow"* (Isaiah 1:18). Sweet friend, God views you as an untarnished blank canvas. Let's no longer keep an inventory of all our mistakes. If we keep account, may it only be of His great love that's wiped it all clean.

EXTRA VERSES FOR STUDY OR PRAYER
Isaiah 1:18; Colossians 3:13

VERSE OF THE DAY

As high as the heavens are above the earth, so great is his love for those who fear him; as far as the east is from the west, so far has he removed our transgressions from us. —Psalm 103:11–12

PRAYER

Lord, thank You for pardoning me for my sins and erasing their very existence. Please help me accept Your mercy, absolve myself, and release those in my life who have hurt me. Produce in me a generous attitude of grace toward others the way You have extended it to me. Show me if there's someone in my life whom I have hurt and give me the strength to humbly ask them for their forgiveness. Help us all to see our lives as a blank canvas like You do. In Jesus's name, amen.

THINK

_____

_____

_____

PRAY

_____

_____

_____

PRAISE

_____

_____

_____

TO-DO   PRAYER LIST

_____   _____

_____   _____

QUESTIONS FOR DEEPER REFLECTION

1. Are you prone to hold on to your trespasses and those who have trespassed against you?

_____

_____

_____

2. How does knowing God has forgiven and forgotten your sins make you feel? How does that compel you to extend that same grace to the people in your life?

_____

_____

_____

DAY 11

LOVE DOES NOT DELIGHT IN EVIL BUT REJOICES WITH TRUTH

Rather, speaking the truth in love, we are to grow up in every way into him who is the head, into Christ.
—Ephesians 4:15 (ESV)

I left the party with a sick feeling in the pit of my stomach. The next day, I was still convicted about the previous night's activities. I hate conflict and am a peacemaker by nature. It was wildly out of my character, but I couldn't shake the feeling I needed to contact the host of the event. I did not want to make the call, but I sensed I would be disobedient to the Lord if I didn't. Not to mention, it would have been "the elephant in the room" for me every time I saw one of the attendees if I didn't get it off my chest.

So with sweaty palms and a shaky voice, I made the call to share my convictions. I explained that I felt like people should be able to see a difference between Christians and non-Christians because of the way we live. I acknowledged that the Christian life is a process, but since we are followers of Christ, we are called to leave behind the old life of sin and be committed to holy living. As gently as possible, I challenged us to ensure our actions reflected Christ's integrity.

After I finished explaining my heart and convictions, I paused to hear her response. She briefly hesitated, digesting what was said, then responded, "You're right, and I'm sorry. We should hold ourselves to a higher standard. Thank you for holding us accountable." I let out a sigh of relief as we continued our discussion. Was it an awkward conversation? Yes. But was I glad I listened to the *"Spirit of truth"* (John 16:13), Who convicted my heart and guided me to speak the truth in love to my friends? Yes. Because I care for my friends, and I want them to lead lives pleasing to the Lord. This is what I desire for them, and this is what I hope for myself.

Even though it is uncomfortable, I have trusted family and friends who hold me accountable. We need others who will encourage and build us up but challenge and call us out when we aren't living up to our God-given potential. The reality is we are all sinful beings who need help. Great people who submit their lives to God are still susceptible to temptation and sin. While Jesus is *"the truth"* (John 14:6), Satan is *"the father of lies"* (John 8:44). Because of this constant tension, we need one another and God's Word to fight this ongoing spiritual battle.

SOMETHING TO THINK ABOUT

A pillar of the Old Testament, David was all too familiar with this struggle. He was renowned and respected for his heart for God. Unfortunately, he was also remembered as a betrayer, liar, adulterer, and murderer. His life reminds us that none of us are immune to falling short and doing evil in the sight of the Lord. When David's actions became wayward, a prophet helped him recollect the truth and repent.

After restoring the nation to peace and great military power, David's life became entangled in sin. He committed adultery with a woman named Bathsheba and then ordered her husband killed in an attempted cover-up. (See 2 Samuel 11.) The prophet Nathan confronted David's sins and helped him see his wrongdoing. (See 2 Samuel 12:1–10.) Nathan served as God's spokesman to David and proved himself a fearless friend and counselor. He was willing to speak the truth, though fully aware of the great pain that could ensue.

As a result of Nathan's intervention, David repented. David wrote Psalm 51 after Nathan confronted him. This psalm reveals

David's sorrow and remorse for the decisions he made. Nathan's courage to speak truth to David led to restoration and a right relationship with God. We too need wise advisors to come alongside us to help us assess our actions and situations.

If you don't have a friend like Nathan, pray for one. Moreover, ask God to use you as a Nathan for someone else. We should not be afraid to tell the truth to those we care about. A trustworthy companion is one of God's greatest gifts. God cares enough to communicate with us, even when we're wrong. Once we realize the truth, He offers us forgiveness and grace because of His great love.

EXTRA VERSES FOR STUDY OR PRAYER
Psalm 1:1–2; 2 Samuel 11 and 12

VERSE OF THE DAY

Rather, speaking the truth in love, we are to grow up in every way into him who is the head, into Christ.

—Ephesians 4:15 (ESV)

PRAYER

Father, guide and teach me what is true. Implant Your truth in my heart so I am not deceived by the lies of the world and the enemy's schemes. Remove any apathy I may have for the behavior of others and give me the courage to sharpen the people in my life *"as iron sharpens iron"* (Proverbs 27:17). If You are leading me to intervene, let my words be filled with grace and love. May I also be open to receiving advice from others. Please place people around me to remind me of Your Word and hold me accountable. In Jesus's name, amen.

THINK

PRAY

_____

_____

_____

PRAISE

_____

_____

TO-DO   PRAYER LIST

_____   _____

_____   _____

_____   _____

QUESTIONS FOR DEEPER REFLECTION

1. When has someone approached you to speak the truth in love to you? How did you receive their intervention?

_____

_____

2. Have you ever approached someone to help sharpen them? How was it received? If not, what stops you from speaking up?

_____

_____

DAY 12

LOVE ALWAYS PROTECTS

Above all, love each other deeply,
because love covers over a multitude of sins.
—1 Peter 4:8

When my daughter Kate was in preschool, she gave my husband Bryan a Father's Day gift we still treasure. The heart-shaped, paper cutout prompted her to fill in the blanks about what she loved about her father. In one of these blanks, she wrote that her dad protected her. Even at such a young age, Kate recognized she felt safe with her father.

I'm so thankful my daughter feels this way about her father. Don't we all long for this kind of safe place—a space where we feel loved for who we are, a place where we don't have to pretend, where we can relax and be transparent? To be entirely known and still be fully loved is one of our ultimate desires, right? Maybe you have been fortunate enough to have this experience with your family or friends. Perhaps you haven't. You may feel the exact opposite. Whatever your reality, I hope you take comfort in knowing you have a heavenly Father with whom you can feel safe, whose love protects you.

As we continue our journey through 1 Corinthians 13:4–8, we read that God's love *"always protects"* in the New International Version (NIV) translation of verse 7, but some other Bible translations say, *"Love bears all things"* (ESV). Upon first reading, the concept of love bearing all things seems to communicate the need for patient endurance. However, in the original Greek language, the word translated as "to bear" (*stegó*) means "to cover closely, to bear up under."[4]

Ever since Genesis in the garden of Eden, God's love has always covered us. When Adam and Eve sinned, they hid and made coverings out of fig leaves to conceal their nakedness. But God, in His loving-kindness, didn't want them to feel ashamed. Instead, He clothed them with "*garments of skin*" (Genesis 3:21). Some Biblical scholars believe these garments must have originated from a sacrificed animal—the shedding of blood to atone for their sin from the very beginning.

SOMETHING TO THINK ABOUT

We also hide in shame and attempt to disguise our sins. Thankfully, God redeems our disgrace and envelops us with His love. Even more unfathomably, Jesus endured our humiliation on the cross. He was the offering instead of an animal sacrifice mentioned in the Old Testament. He was "*pierced for our transgressions*" and "*crushed for our iniquities*" (Isaiah 53:5) to absolve all our sins. (See Psalm 85:2.) Jesus bore our due penalty so that we would have the freedom to "*live for righteousness*" (1 Peter 2:24).

When Jesus died in our place, we were spared the punishment we deserved. This is called substitutionary atonement. The original Hebrew word for "atonement" is *kaphar*, which also means "to cover over."[5] Jesus could have protected Himself from the pain on the cross. Yet He *chose* to suffer for our sakes so that we would be acceptable to God. What can we say to such love? Better yet, what will we do with such love?

One of Jesus's twelve disciples gives us a good place to start. Peter says, "*Above all, love each other deeply, because love **covers over** a multitude of sins*" (1 Peter 4:8). This doesn't mean we brush our feelings under the rug or allow sin to remain unaddressed. We should acknowledge trespasses, then extend forgiveness to ourselves and others that God has mercifully bestowed upon us. His love covers a multitude of sins, not ours. It is His grace that is tangibly expressed

---

4. 4722. stegó. *Strong's Greek Concordance.*
5. 3722. kaphar. *Strong's Hebrew Concordance.*

through us. Our hatred only stirs up dissension, but God's love *"covers over all wrongs"* (Proverbs 10:12). None of us are without failures, but we are all blanketed by His blood. This gives us security both now and for eternity.

I don't know how you would fill in the blank of your heart-shaped paper cutout if you were to notate the treasured qualities of your earthly father. But I do know how we can all fill in the blank about our heavenly Father: His love will always protect us. You can take refuge in the shelter of His wings, for the Lord is your strength and shield. (See, respectively, Psalms 91:4, 28:7.) His love is always available to guard you and make you feel secure.

EXTRA VERSES FOR STUDY OR PRAYER

Psalm 28:7; Psalm 91:4

VERSE OF THE DAY

Above all, love each other deeply, because love covers over a multitude of sins.

—1 Peter 4:8

PRAYER

Father, I am grateful for how You protect me physically, many times without me realizing it. Thank You, Jesus, for covering my sin and shame with Your blood on the cross. May I never take for granted Your atoning sacrifice on my behalf. Maintain a hedge of protection around me and those I love. Keep us safe. Help me to lead others into the safety of Your arms to be covered by Your love. In Jesus's name, amen.

THINK

_____

_____

_____

PRAY

_____

_____

_____

PRAISE

_____

_____

_____

TO-DO   ## PRAYER LIST

_____   _____

_____   _____

_____   _____

QUESTIONS FOR DEEPER REFLECTION

1. Have you ever felt unsafe? Where were you and who was there?
    On the flip side, where or with whom do you feel safest?

_____

_____

2. Who needs a spiritual, emotional, or physical safe space that you
    might be able to provide?

_____

_____

_____

DAY 13

LOVE ALWAYS TRUSTS

Trust in the LORD with all your heart and lean not on your own understanding; in all your ways submit to him, and he will make your paths straight.
—Proverbs 3:5–6

I remember attending a *Women of Joy* conference where Dave Ramsey and his daughter, Rachel Ramsey Cruze, delivered a keynote address on parenting. Dave talked about learning to trust your child as you gain confidence in their choices and behaviors. He spoke metaphorically of a rope tied to a child while a parent holds the end of the rope. As the child makes good decisions, they receive more rope. If poor choices occur, the parent pulls the child closer to keep them safe until confidence is restored.

What was so special about this example was how Dave shared that he gave Rachel a rope as a gift when she married. This gift symbolized his belief in her and served as a tangible reminder of that. I've never forgotten this endearing image, especially as I began parenting my children. It amazes me how God has entrusted me to care for them. He has also asked you to care for something or someone. He charges us to love others and holds us accountable to steward specific roles. But we need His help to fulfill these responsibilities. Relying on God allows us to care for what He has entrusted to us. (See 2 Timothy 1:14.)

It takes a long time to develop trust in others and just seconds to lose it. However, Paul writes that love *"always trusts"* (1 Corinthians 13:7). So often, we place our confidence or trust in earthly things—other people, wealth, position, talent, and even ourselves. But all of these can fail us. God is the only entity in heaven and on earth worthy of our complete reliance.

SOMETHING TO THINK ABOUT

Trustworthiness can be measured by a person's follow-through in keeping their word. God, as *the* Word, establishes the standard for this metric. Scripture tells us in John 1:1, *"In the beginning was the Word, and the Word was with God, and the Word was God."* God has always honored His covenants. Throughout Scripture, God has proven that what He says is *"trustworthy and true"* (Revelation 21:5).

Bible scholars have estimated there are approximately 8,810 promises in Scripture.[6] When Jesus came to live as Immanuel, God with us, He fulfilled more than three hundred biblical prophecies written between five hundred and one thousand years before Jesus was born. The mathematical probability of one person fulfilling just eight prophesies is one in a hundred million billion.[7]

Doesn't this strengthen your faith when you understand the depth of God's assurances? First Corinthians 13:7 (ESV) tells us that love *"believes all things."* When we bear witness to the actualization of God's promises, it bolsters our belief in His love for us too. Since He promises to love us *"with an everlasting love"* (Jeremiah 31:3), we can take Him at His word.

The difficulty comes when we experience hard seasons when God's timelines or outcomes don't align with ours, or when He's asking us to obey and His plan doesn't make sense. However, in these instances, God is giving us a little rope, beckoning us to trust Him and allowing our faith to grow.

Regardless of our circumstances, He is asking us to believe. God knows and wants what is best for us far more than we ever could. His ways are higher than ours, and His thoughts are higher than

---

6. Everek R. Storms, "God's Promises," Interchurch Holiness Convention, August 24, 2021, ihconvention.com/convention-herald/gods-promises.
7. Lee Strobel, *The Case for Christ: A Journalist's Personal Investigation of the Evidence for Jesus* (Grand Rapids, MI: Zondervan, 1998), 246.

our thoughts. (See Isaiah 55:9.) We may not have all the answers in this life, but each experience allows us to learn to trust Him with all our heart and not rely on our own understanding, knowing that the longer we walk with Him, the stronger our faith becomes.

While our reliance upon Him continues to grow, I don't think God ever intends to give us the entire rope. We will always need to depend on His leading. I pray we are tethered so closely to Him that we hear the cadence of His voice and sense every movement to stay near Him forever—especially as we care for what has been entrusted to us. He is true to His Word. He has demonstrated His faithfulness, and His love can be trusted.

EXTRA VERSES FOR STUDY OR PRAYER
Isaiah 55:9; Revelation 21:5

VERSE OF THE DAY

Trust in the LORD with all your heart and lean not on your own understanding; in all your ways submit to him, and he will make your paths straight.   —Proverbs 3:5–6

PRAYER

Father, thank You for being trustworthy and true. I want to trust You and Your love for me. Help me to believe Your plans for me are good. When my faith is stretched, I pray I cling tightly to You and Your promises. Forgive me for acting inauthentically. May I be a person others can depend on to lead them into a closer relationship with You. In Jesus's name, amen.

THINK

_____

_____

_____

PRAY

_____

_____

PRAISE

_____

_____

_____

TO-DO   PRAYER LIST

_____   _____

_____   _____

_____   _____

QUESTIONS FOR DEEPER REFLECTION

1. Is your reliance and dependence on the people and things of this world or on the Lord? What circumstance or situation do you need to trust Him in right now?

_____

_____

2. Who in your life do you trust most? How could you be a more trustworthy person?

_____

_____

_____

DAY 14

LOVE ALWAYS HOPES

The Lord delights in those who fear him,
who put their hope in his unfailing love.
—Psalm 147:11

I've always been a bit of a hopeless romantic, an enduring believer in happily ever after. Perhaps it stems back to Disney movies about princesses who marry a Prince Charming riding in on his white horse. *Brides* magazine assures me I'm not alone in my utopian notions. It reports that hopeless romantics "choose to see the positive in relationships over the negative, believing wholeheartedly that love conquers all." They are "more susceptible to falling in love" and get "carried away in their romantic feelings."[8] Yes, these words describe me to a T.

I tend to walk around wearing rose-colored glasses. I'm the one in our marriage who will always choose the outdoor seating at restaurants, knowing it's sweltering hot, and our food will be swarming with bugs before the meal ends. Or the person in our family who wants to go to the orchard to get our caramel apples and the pumpkin patch to purchase our mums each fall. And, of course, each winter, I insist that we drive around to see the Christmas lights while sipping hot chocolate and listening to carols to create traditions and memories ... even if my family rolls their eyes at me every year.

Many of us hope and pray for world peace, but as we read the latest headlines and watch the news, it seems unrealistic, like a fairy tale that will never come true.

---

8. Cristina Montemayor, "What Is a Hopeless Romantic? 11 Signs You Might Be One," *Brides* magazine, October 3, 2023, www.brides.com/what-is-a-hopeless-romantic-5095882.

There is a lot we desire to be different—unanswered prayers we've been waiting and longing for. We pray for open doors and new opportunities, a better economy, adequate work, cures for diseases, significant others to propose, positive pregnancy tests, and loved ones to come to believe in Christ. How many times have your hopes been raised only to see them crushed? Even the most optimistic personalities can become worn out and weary trying to hold on to hope.

SOMETHING TO THINK ABOUT

Sisters Mary and Martha experienced hopelessness when their brother Lazarus was ill. They sent word to Jesus, *"Lord, the one you love is sick"* (John 11:3). When Jesus heard this, He responded, *"This sickness will not end in death. No, it is for God's glory so that God's Son may be glorified through it"* (John 11:4). Scripture records that Jesus loved the siblings, yet He did not go to heal Lazarus for two more days. He knew their pain but didn't respond immediately. His delay had a purpose.

When Jesus arrived, Lazarus had been in the tomb for four days. Mary and Martha both cried out to Jesus in their anguish, "If You had been here, Lazarus would not have died!" (See John 11:21, 32.) Jesus wept at the tomb, and the Jews remarked about how much He cared for Lazarus. Deeply moved, Jesus commanded that the stone be rolled away from the entrance. Then He prayed and called for Lazarus—and the dead man walked out of the grave. When all hope seemed lost, Jesus performed a miracle.

It wasn't long after this experience that Jesus Himself was in the tomb. I imagine the disciples felt hopeless in the hours between Jesus's death and His resurrection. Their hearts must have been overcome with doubt and sorrow on Holy Saturday, the day between Good Friday and Easter Sunday. Every promise they clung to was buried in a grave.

Life feels this way sometimes, doesn't it? God's timing, especially His delays, may make us think He is not answering or responding in the way we want. But He will meet all our needs according to His perfect schedule and purpose. We must simply wait on Him.

Despite my faith-filled expectations, I feel the heaviness of life in this world too. Thankfully, I also see the light at the end of the tunnel. In the midst of all the desperation is a thrill of hope, and His name is Jesus. The people in the Old Testament were longing for a Savior. Then, on a starry night in Bethlehem, love came down to this weary world as a baby in a manger. He changed the lives of all who encountered Him. He isn't Prince Charming on a white horse, but He is the King of Kings and Lord of Lords who made His triumphal entry into Jerusalem on a donkey. (See Matthew 21:7.) And one day, He will return to earth for a second and final time. (See Revelation 1:7.) With this hope, we can rejoice no matter how much tribulation we face.

EXTRA VERSES FOR STUDY OR PRAYER

Mark 9:23; Romans 8:24–25

VERSE OF THE DAY

The Lord delights in those who fear him, who put their hope in his unfailing love.   —Psalm 147:11

PRAYER

Father, the world around me can cause me to feel hopeless. In situations when I've been praying and waiting on Your answer, help me to trust in Your plan and timing. I put my hope in You and believe You are in control. Fill my heart and mind with faith to live optimistically based on the promises in Your Word. In Jesus's name, amen.

THINK

_____

_____

_____

PRAY

_____

_____

_____

PRAISE

_____

_____

_____

TO-DO

_____

_____

_____

PRAYER LIST

_____

_____

_____

QUESTIONS FOR DEEPER REFLECTION

1. Would you consider yourself an optimistic or a pessimistic person? If you are feeling hopeless, how can you recapture the feeling of hope?

_____

_____

_____

2. How can having a sense of hope make life better for you and those around you?

_____

_____

_____

DAY 15

LOVE ALWAYS PERSEVERES

[Love] *always perseveres.*
—1 Corinthians 13:7

As I faced Bryan in my white dress, my eyes were locked on his. Holding on to each other's newly ringed hands, we listened as his grandparents read 1 Corinthians 13 from their tattered Bible. At the time of our wedding, Norman and Anne had been married for fifty-one years. As they quoted each love quality, I knew the words were more than lip service. Their marriage was a living testament to each characteristic. As I said "I do" before God, family, and friends, I was inspired by what they had done—how they had lived out their commitment.

As time passed, Alzheimer's disease overtook Norman's mind. Anne made the difficult decision to move from their family home of fifty-four years to reside in a nursing home. Norman was over six feet tall, and Anne was around five feet tall, so it was difficult for her to care for him as needed. Anne was healthy in body and mind, but she chose to move into the nursing home with Norman so they could remain together.

She cared for him like she always had: laying out his clothes, changing his socks, ensuring he had his medications, and making sure he had the food required for his diabetes. They'd sit together in one room, talking, reading, watching television, sharing meals, and occasionally walking around the block. Her devotion to him and selfless love still moves me. She could have lived separately from him for more freedom but chose to stay regardless of the less-than-ideal living situation.

Norman has gone on to be with the Lord, but his legacy lives on through his daughters, grandchildren, and great-grandchildren. When he passed, he and Anne had been married for sixty-eight years. It's been five years since he passed, but Anne still wears her wedding ring. Their love wasn't perfect, but it persevered and lives on in Anne today.

The Bible beside me as I write this devotion was a gift from Bryan's grandparents on our wedding day. Our names are embossed in gold on the front. On the first page, they signed and dated it with Psalm 119:105 (ESV) written underneath: "*Your word is a lamp to my feet and a light to my path.*" Such true words from two people who persevered as faithful examples and guides.

SOMETHING TO THINK ABOUT

Where you go I will go, and where you stay I will stay. Your people will be my people and your God my God. Where you die I will die, and there I will be buried. May the LORD deal with me, be it ever so severely, if even death separates you and me.
—Ruth 1:16–17

These words remind me of Norman and Anne but were spoken by Ruth to her mother-in-law, Naomi.

When we first meet these two biblical characters, they are destitute widows. In the ancient world, widows were taken advantage of, ignored, and almost always impoverished. Because of their plight, Naomi decided to return to Israel to find relatives to help her. Despite her desperate situation, Naomi encouraged Ruth and her other daughter-in-law, Orpah, to stay in Moab and restart their lives. She realized this would mean more hardship for her, yet she acted selflessly on behalf of her family. Orpah kissed her mother-in-law goodbye, but Ruth remained with Naomi despite having to leave her homeland.

So the women set out together for Bethlehem in Judah. This unlikely pair came from different cultures and family backgrounds, but they were bound to each other. They shared deep sorrow and great affection for one another. Their greatest bond was faith in God and a commitment to doing what was best for the other.

They made their home in Bethlehem. Because they were widows, they had no means of providing for themselves, so Ruth went into the fields to glean grain, gathering up what was left over by the harvesters. In the following months, God led Ruth to a man named Boaz, whom she eventually married. As a result, she became the great-grandmother of David and an ancestor of Jesus.

Ruth and Naomi's relationship is a beautiful example of perseverance, friendship, and allegiance. As a result of faithful obedience, their lives and legacies were significant even though they could not personally see the fruit of their labor.

When we live faithfully, our significance will extend beyond our lifetime too. Future generations benefit when we persist and don't give up on our relationships. Just as Ruth and Naomi were unaware of the larger purpose for their lives, we will not know our lives' full objective and impact until eternity. Therefore, we should make decisions with God's everlasting values in mind and not take moral shortcuts for short-term pleasures. The rewards will far exceed any sacrifice we make.

EXTRA VERSES FOR STUDY OR PRAYER
Hebrews 10:36; Hebrews 12:1–2

VERSE OF THE DAY

[Love] *always perseveres.*   —1 Corinthians 13:7

PRAYER

Father, forgive me for giving up on people too soon. Give me the courage and endurance to be loyal and faithful. When it is Your desire, help me to stay when I want to leave. Thank You for persisting in Your relationship with me. I'm grateful You will never leave me or forsake me. In Jesus's name, amen.

THINK

_____
_____
_____

PRAY

_____
_____
_____

PRAISE

_____
_____
_____

TO-DO   PRAYER LIST

_____   _____
_____   _____
_____   _____

QUESTIONS FOR DEEPER REFLECTION

1. Is there a relationship you have given up on? How can you perse-
    vere to stay rather than leave?

_____
_____
_____

2. Think of someone whose relationships you admire. How can you
    mimic the qualities and characteristics they've modeled in your
    own life?

_____
_____
_____

DAY 16

LOVE NEVER FAILS

Praise the LORD! He is good. God's love never fails.
—Psalm 136:1 (CEV)

I received my first Valentine's Day gift in fifth grade. I nervously approached my "boyfriend" and handed him the mixed tape I'd worked hard to compile with what I considered to be the perfect playlist. In return, he handed me a heart-shaped box of chocolates.

"I was a little hungry, so I ate a few," he sheepishly admitted. To my dismay, I slowly opened the red-foiled container ... only to discover a remnant of chocolates left. I can laugh about it now, but my childhood heart felt empty at that moment. His lack of care for my feelings was evident in his actions. Needless to say, that relationship didn't last long.

I imagine your heart has also been broken more than a time or two in this life. Human love has failed us and triggered so much pain. It's likely that we have also caused heartache by our lack of loving actions. Every affection we hoped to receive on earth has come up short of perfection because we are fallen, sinful beings. Our unmet expectations leave us with unfulfilled hopes for what is possible. Due to our hurtful experiences, we have a tainted understanding of love. Consequently, we have difficulty grasping the concept that God's love is *"everlasting"* (Jeremiah 31:3).

When we struggle to see the evidence of God's adoration in our lives, it is helpful to read accounts of His loving presence in the lives of our biblical ancestors. Scripture is the story of the Lord's love for mankind. Psalm 136 provides one of the most concise examples of His faithfulness to humanity. The Contemporary English Version of the chapter repeats, *"God's love never fails"* twenty-six times—in each verse—after recounting God's provision for the people in the Old Testament. The author of this psalm is anonymous, but scholars have concluded it may have been a responsive reading, with the assembly saying these words in unison after each sentence. While the repetition helped engrain this conviction in the hearts of these ancient congregations, it is a timeless truth we must also take to heart.

SOMETHING TO THINK ABOUT

Since God's love never failed our forefathers, we can be confident that it won't let us down either. In a world of constant change, God says, *"I never change"* (Malachi 3:6 CEV). *"He is the same yesterday, today, and forever"* (Hebrews 13:8 CEV). In other words, God has been and will be the same for all eternity. He is *"I AM"* (Exodus 3:14)—endless and constant. So if we believe God's presence is continuous—meaning that He was, is, and will be—then we can also trust His affection is inexhaustible toward us.

It's helpful to reflect on our lives and consider how God has displayed His infallible devotion to us. Try making a list of all the ways you've experienced evidence of His presence in your life. Then, after each statement, write, "God's love never fails." Let this sentence become a mantra to remind you, *"Because of the LORD's great love we are not consumed, for his compassions never fail. They are new every morning; great is your faithfulness"* (Lamentations 3:22–23).

If you feel empty today and disappointed by the absence of love from the people in your life, I can empathize. Our hearts have an insatiable longing that always seems to remain unfulfilled. Only God is capable of filling the void. Allow God to saturate you with abundance to the point you are overflowing into the life of others. (See, respectively, Ephesians 3:19; 1 Thessalonians 3:12.) We never have to worry that He will run out of love because it flows from a well that will never dry.

EXTRA VERSES FOR STUDY OR PRAYER

Ephesians 3:19; 1 Thessalonians 3:12

VERSE OF THE DAY

Praise the Lord! He is good. God's love never fails.
                                   —Psalm 136:1 (CEV)

PRAYER

Father, heal my broken heart. I've been hurt by the people in my life who have let me down. Help me to forgive them. I also acknowledge that I have caused heartache. For that, I am sorry. Make my heart more like Yours. Remind me of the ways You have exhibited Your affection for me. I don't want to go to anyone else looking for the love only You can give. Thank You for being steadfast and never failing me. In Jesus's name, amen.

THINK

_____

_____

_____

PRAY

_____

_____

_____

PRAISE

_____

_____

TO-DO   PRAYER LIST

_____   _____

_____   _____

QUESTIONS FOR DEEPER REFLECTION

1. Does your heart feel empty or full? Where do you usually go to fill up when you feel void of love?

    _____

    _____

2. Do you believe God's love never fails? Has He ever failed you? Think about the ways God has been faithful to you.

    _____

    _____

    _____

PART TWO

LIVING OUT LOVE

DAY 17

LOVING DEPENDENTLY

As the Father has loved me, so have I loved you.
Now remain in my love.
—John 15:9

Not long ago, I purchased a Bible for a friend who doubted God's love and highlighted all the times Scripture mentioned the word. When I began this task, I did not realize that according to the New International Version, the word appears 686 times![9] God didn't just want my friend to realize His love for her; He wanted me to comprehend it too! The repetition alone clearly demonstrates the importance of this message. No wonder the Bible is regularly referred to as *God's love letter*.

However, we can easily miss the realization of His love for us if we don't spend time with Him. A friend of mine equates this to going on a date with a man who knows your potential mate in order to get to know your future husband. We would never do that! We must spend quality time with our significant others to feel close to them. This concept applies to any relationship in our lives—including our relationship with God. While devotionals like this one and many other books from well-intentioned authors are great resources to help us grasp biblical concepts and broaden our thinking, we must also go straight to the source: God's Word. If we want to feel connected to God, it's essential we abide with Him through Scripture reading, prayer, and worship.

Continuing the dating analogy, how strong would your relationship be with your significant other or a friend if you only spent five

9. "686 Bible results for 'love' from New International Version," www.biblegateway.com/quicksearch/?quicksearch=love&version=NIV.

minutes each day talking with them? You wouldn't feel very connected, would you? Likewise, if you only spend five minutes a day with God, you probably will not feel a deep bond with Him either. While I know we are all busy, what would transpire if you spent thirty minutes, an hour, or more with God every day? Imagine the impact on your relationship with Him and how that might transform your life.

I want to be clear—I don't always get this right. I'm guilty of working *for* God and considering that time spent *with* God. Recently, I was getting up early to write devotions. I'd heard your most productive writing occurs early in the morning because your mind is clear and more creative. However, I found that I lacked inspiration after several weeks of practicing this new routine. I was putting in the work but wasn't bearing much fruit.

At this realization, a verse from Scripture popped into my head:

If you remain in me and I in you, you will bear much fruit; apart from me you can do nothing.   —John 15:5

With a sting of conviction, I changed my morning routine back to being with Him first. When I began my day communing with God, I noticed a change in my heart and mind, affecting my actions and behaviors. My family could tell the difference too! This doesn't mean we need to get legalistic about our spiritual disciplines. There is grace in this process, but there is also a blessing. Time spent with God is never time wasted.

We don't have to stop our communion with God after time spent reading His Word. We can continue to dwell with Him by playing worship music in the car, while exercising, or doing chores. We can also talk to Him all day. In an interview with Rachel Wojo on *The Love Offering* podcast, she shared that she doesn't say "amen" at the end of her morning prayers because she wants to keep the conversation with God going all day long. Before bed, she finally says "amen."[10] Don't you just love that? We can abide with Christ throughout the day.

---

10. "A Little Healing Goes a Long Way with Rachel Wojo," *The Love Offering* podcast, Season 5 Episode 45, November 21, 2023, podcasters.spotify.com/pod/show/theloveoffering/episodes/A-Little-Healing-Goes-a-Long-Way-with-Rachel-Wojo-e2alnba.

SOMETHING TO THINK ABOUT

To *abide* means "to remain" or "to stay." Jesus illustrates an abiding relationship with Him through the parable of the vine and the branches. In this parable, Christ is the vine and God is the gardener who cares for the branches (us) to make them fruitful. Apart from Christ, our efforts will be in vain.

Fruit is not limited to soul winning. *"The fruit of the Spirit is love, joy, peace, patience, kindness, goodness, faithfulness, gentleness, [and] self-control"* (Galatians 5:22–23 ESV). The Holy Spirit produces these character traits, but if we desire the fruit of the Spirit to grow in us, we must join our lives to His.

Many of us want the abundance God offers, but we are unwilling to put forth the effort to improve our intimacy with Him. Experiencing God, doing His will, developing perseverance, and loving others does not come automatically; they require hard work. God empowers and enables us, but He gives us the task to learn and grow. Unfathomably, He has chosen and appointed us to *"go and bear fruit—fruit that will last"* (John 15:16). What a privilege and responsibility it is to abide in communion with Him.

EXTRA VERSES FOR STUDY OR PRAYER

Galatians 5:22–23; 2 Peter 1:5–8

VERSE OF THE DAY

As the Father has loved me, so have I loved you. Now remain in my love.   —John 15:9

PRAYER

Father, I am grateful I get to commune with You. Thank You for allowing me to abide in You. Remind me that apart from You, I can do nothing, but with You, nothing is impossible. Help me to stay connected with You so I may bear much fruit. I want my life to bring forth abundance for Your kingdom and Your glory. In Jesus's name, amen.

THINK

_____

_____

_____

PRAY

_____

_____

_____

PRAISE

_____

_____

TO-DO   PRAYER LIST

_____   _____

_____   _____

_____   _____

QUESTIONS FOR DEEPER REFLECTION

1. Are you receiving the nourishment and life offered by Christ, the vine? What intentional steps can you take to dwell with Him each day?

_____

_____

_____

2. Is your life producing fruit? Which of the fruit of the Spirit do
    you need God to grow in you?

    _____

    _____

    _____

DAY 18

LOVING
WHOLEHEARTEDLY

Yet I hold this against you:
You have forsaken the love you had at first.
—Revelation 2:4

Who was your first love? Not long ago, I was rummaging through my old yearbooks and came across one from elementary school. My first crush had written on one of the blank pages, "I don't know what else to say, but I love you." I laughed out loud when I saw his childish proclamation. I giggled even more when I noticed I had returned the youthful sentiments in the margins of my notebooks. Young love, right? I thought I felt this way about him. Maybe I did, based on the limited understanding of my naive heart. But as I grew older and met my husband, Bryan, what I know now of love is much different than what I knew then. The notes written by Bryan and his words of endearment hold a much deeper meaning than those from my youth.

Even within our marriage, our affection has grown since we first met. And while devotion has increased over the past twenty years of our relationship, we must be diligent to continually seek ways to make each other feel special. We were first together in college, so we had fewer responsibilities and focusing solely on one another was simpler. But over time, as we've purchased homes, started businesses, and had children, our attention has become more divided. As the years have passed, we have found that it takes intentional effort from both of us to ensure we continue prioritizing our marriage.

The same is true of everyone's relationship with the Lord. When we first encounter Him, we are filled with awe and zeal. We can't wait to be in His presence, pray, attend church, worship, and read our Bibles. But then, over the years, if we aren't careful, our feelings can grow stale, and we can forget the magnitude of what He means to us.

SOMETHING TO THINK ABOUT

This was the case for the church of Ephesus. In Paul's letter to the Ephesians around AD 60, the apostle commended them for their fervent love and faith: *"Ever since I heard about your faith in the Lord Jesus and your love for all God's people, I have not stopped giving thanks for you, remembering you in my prayers"* (Ephesians 1:15–16).

However, thirty-five years later when the apostle John writes a letter to the same church notated in the book of Revelation, it carries a much different tone. He tells the Ephesians:

> *I know your deeds, your hard work and your perseverance. …*
> *You have persevered and have endured hardships for my name,*
> *and have not grown weary. Yet I hold this against you: You have*
> *forsaken the love you had at first. Consider how far you have*
> *fallen! Repent and do the things you did at first.*
> —Revelation 2:2–5

Many of the church founders had died by the time this letter was written, and numerous second-generation believers had lost their passion for God. They were a busy church, but they were no longer motivated by their love for God. Perhaps outside influences, the things of this world, or a focus on ministry over devotion had caused their love to fracture.

The Creator *"is a jealous God"* (Exodus 34:14); He wants our whole hearts. However, He knew we would be prone to wander; therefore, He promised, *"I will give them an undivided heart and put a new spirit in them; I will remove from them their heart of stone and give them a heart of flesh"* (Ezekiel 11:19).

This heart transplant is the work of the Holy Spirit. To exchange stubborn hearts of stone for responsive hearts of flesh is the work of a loving God with a tenderness toward His creation—and a soft spot particularly for you. In fact, Scripture reveals, *"The eyes of the Lord run to and fro throughout the whole earth, to give strong support to those whose heart is blameless toward him"* (2 Chronicles 16:9 ESV).

Do you long to love God with all your heart? If this is your desire, follow David's example and pray:

> *Teach me your way, O Lord, that I may walk in your truth; unite my heart to fear your name. I give thanks to you, O Lord my God, with my whole heart, and I will glorify your name forever. For great is your steadfast love toward me.*
>
> —Psalm 86:11–13 ESV

Let us not forsake our first love. Instead, may God grant us the ability to be faithful to the end. Allow this hymn to minister to your heart and give voice to our prayer:

> *Prone to wander, Lord, I feel it,*
> *Prone to leave the God I love;*
> *Here's my heart, O take and seal it,*
> *Seal it for Thy courts above.*[11]

EXTRA VERSES FOR STUDY OR PRAYER

Ephesians 1:15–16; Revelation 2:2–4

VERSE OF THE DAY

Yet I hold this against you: You have forsaken the love you had at first.
                                        —Revelation 2:4

PRAYER

Father, You are my first love. Help me to keep You as the highest importance in my life. Forgive me for ever having

---

11. Robert Robinson, "Come, Thou Fount of Every Blessing, 1758.

a divided heart. When I get distracted or chase after any other loves, draw me back to You. May I display my affection and intention for You with even more enthusiasm than at the beginning of our relationship. Thank You for loving me wholeheartedly. In Jesus's name, amen.

THINK

_____

_____

PRAY

_____

_____

PRAISE

_____

_____

TO-DO

_____

_____

_____

PRAYER LIST

_____

_____

_____

QUESTIONS FOR DEEPER REFLECTION

1. Do you love God with the same fervor as you did in your early days as a new Christian? How has your relationship changed and developed over the years?

    _____

    _____

    _____

2. Who or what do you love more than God right now? If your heart has been divided, how can you make God a priority again?

    _____

    _____

    _____

DAY 19

LOVING FEARLESSLY

There is no fear in love. But perfect love drives out fear.
—1 John 4:18

I didn't want to put myself out there again. Every time I did, I was met with disinterest. I already felt like I didn't belong in the group, which seemed to be affirmed each time I brought up an idea or topic of conversation. Whether or not I was misreading the situation, I couldn't shake the feeling that I wasn't enough. So in self-defense, I pulled back. I chose to respond less and withdrew myself from the group before they removed me.

We tend to self-protect when we have been hurt, don't we? Our instinct is to hide or put up walls so our hearts don't get broken. I'm sure we have all had instances when we extended an invitation and were told *no*, tried out for the team and didn't make it, applied for the job and didn't get it, worked toward our dream and were met with a closed door, or gave our best in a relationship and were rejected. In these instances, we are tempted to close ourselves off, never to try again. We allow fear of future failure to prevent us from faithfully moving forward.

While this behavior feels safer, it simply isolates us and makes us more vulnerable. The enemy of our souls *"prowls around like a roaring lion looking for someone to devour"* (1 Peter 5:8). While I'm no zoologist, I'm sure a pack of animals has a much better chance of protecting themselves against a lion than a single animal alone. The same is true for us as believers. There is strength in community.

If that community has caused the hurt, we are tempted to escape. Hiding has been humanity's tendency from the beginning of time. When Adam and Eve ate the forbidden fruit, they hid from God. (See Genesis 3:8.) But what did God do? He pursued them.

Since creation and despite rejection, God has desired to fellowship with mankind, pursuing a closer relationship with us. Throughout Scripture, we see the progression of Him moving toward us. First, His Spirit hovered over the waters. Next, He lived in the desert in the tabernacle. Then God became flesh when Christ came to live on the earth. When Jesus ascended to heaven at Pentecost, He sent the Holy Spirit to come and dwell within us. Isn't it unfathomable that the God of the universe would want to be so near to us? No matter what your earthly relationships are like, God is pursuing you.

SOMETHING TO THINK ABOUT

We learned recently that there are 686 mentions of love in the Bible. Fear also ranks high in biblical word count, with the emotion mentioned 437 times. I've heard it said that God has told us to "fear not" or some variations of the phrase 365 times in His Word—one for each day in the year. He knew we would struggle with these feelings. Fear is a valid emotion we should pay attention to, especially if we are unsafe. However, when we are afraid, we can trust that God will be with us. First John 4:18 says, *"There is no fear in love. But perfect love drives out fear, because fear has to do with punishment. The one who fears is not made perfect in love."* God's love will quiet your fears and give you confidence.

In the Old Testament, a servant of Abraham named Hagar escaped to the desert due to her mistreatment by Abraham's wife Sarah. Despite her attempts to run away, God continued to pursue her in her distress. After this encounter, Hagar called Him *"The God Who Sees Me"* (Genesis 16:13 CEV). Hagar returned and birthed her son, Ishmael. Fourteen years later, Isaac was born to Abraham and Sarah. (See Genesis 21:2.) The bitterness between the two women continued, and Sarah demanded Hagar and Ishmael be cast out. Although it grieved Abraham to do so, he gave Hagar and Ishmael some provisions and sent them away. Once again, God graciously intervened and provided water for them.

This story reminds us that no matter who or where we are, God sees and cares about us. He will comfort and provide for anyone who turns to Him and always keeps His promises.

Escape is only a temporary solution. God continually desires us to face our problems with His help. We experience His aid most clearly in and through conflicts and difficulties, not away from them. Are there problems in your life from which you've been running away? Allow His perfect love to cast out your fear.

EXTRA VERSES FOR STUDY OR PRAYER
Isaiah 41:10; Romans 8:15

VERSE OF THE DAY

There is no fear in love. But perfect love drives out fear.
—1 John 4:18

PRAYER

Father, I admit I'm afraid of the heartbreak that can happen in relationships. I have felt rejected and unwanted by people in my life. It feels safer to stay alone rather than risk being hurt again. But I know You've made me for community. Give me the courage to open my heart again. Remind me that You accept, choose, and see me. I no longer want to live in fear. Cast it out and replace it with Your love. In Jesus's name, amen.

THINK

_____

_____

_____

PRAY

_____

_____

_____

PRAISE

_____

_____

_____

TO-DO   PRAYER LIST

_____   _____

_____   _____

_____   _____

QUESTIONS FOR DEEPER REFLECTION

1. Have you been hurt in relationships with people or even with God? Has this caused you to pull back in self-protection?

_____

_____

2. What could happen if you pushed past the fear? How does knowing God sees you and loves you help to open your heart again?

_____

_____

DAY 20

LOVING UNCONDITIONALLY

Know therefore that the Lord your God is God; he is the faithful God, keeping His covenant of love to a thousand generations of those who love Him and keep his commandments. —Deuteronomy 7:9

As soon as I saw the two pink lines revealed on the little white strip, my heart changed. As my belly expanded and I felt them move, my affection grew. The excitement built as my husband Bryan and I decided on their names, hung up their clothes, and prepared the nursery. Though labor and delivery were painful, holding each of my children in my arms for the first time was worth it all. I'd sit for hours staring at their sweet faces and marveling at those tiny miracles. In these newborn stages, Will and Kate didn't do much of anything except sleep, eat, and cry. Yet I was head over heels in love with them.

It was a long time before Will and Kate reached the age when they could tell me they loved me. The first time they said those three little words and threw their arms around my neck was a feeling I will always cherish. However, it was also around this same age when they started to misbehave. While it was not something we enjoyed, when Bryan and I disciplined them for some of their poor decisions, it was an expression of our care for them.

Will and Kate are teenagers now, and our family of four has experienced many highs and lows. But our love for one another hasn't changed. If anything, it has deepened over time. Regardless of their accomplishments or failures, my love for them has remained steadfast. There is nothing they can do to make me love them more, and nothing they can do to cause me to love them less.

God's affection for us is unconditional too. His feelings don't depend on your attitudes or actions—you are His beloved. Before He formed you in your mother's womb, He adored you. Before you took your first breath, He delighted in you. Regardless of how you fail or succeed, He will never stop cherishing you. Rest assured— you are already loved.

SOMETHING TO THINK ABOUT

Peter, one of the disciples, is a prime example of the Lord's merciful and unconditional love. During the Last Supper, Peter proudly told Jesus, *"I will lay down my life for you"* (John 13:37). But Jesus corrected Peter and told him that very night he would deny his Master to protect himself. (See verse 38.) Later, after Christ's arrest, Peter in his fright did deny knowing Jesus three times. Unable to stand up for his Lord for even twelve hours, he had failed as a disciple and friend. When the rooster crowed, Peter realized what he had done and wept bitterly.

After Jesus died on the cross and was resurrected, He appeared to His disciples, who were fishing on the Sea of Galilee. (See John 21.) As soon as Peter recognized Him, he jumped into the water and swam to Jesus on the shore. The risen Messiah did not scold the disciples for deserting Him. Instead, He prepared breakfast for them. When they finished eating, Jesus spoke to Peter and commissioned him specifically.

Jesus led Peter through an experience that would redeem the regret of his denial. Peter had disowned Jesus three times, so Jesus asked Peter three times if he loved Him. (See John 21:15–17). When Peter answered yes, Jesus told him to feed and care for His sheep. The repetition of three was a symbol of grace applied. Peter did not miss this significance. He repented, and Jesus asked him again to commit his life to the Lord's purposes.

Peter's life changed when he finally realized who Jesus was and that he was forgiven. Peter became an evangelist for Christ and wrote 1 Peter and 2 Peter. In these epistles, Peter knew his death was imminent. Many years before, Christ prepared Peter for the death he would face. (See John 21:18–19.) Jesus's prophecy came true when Peter was martyred for his faith. When the moment came, he did not deny Christ this time. According to one tradition, he was crucified upside down at his request because he did not feel worthy to die in the same manner as the Messiah.

Jesus's first words to Peter were *"Come, follow me"* (Matthew 4:19), and His last words to him were *"You must follow me"* (John 21:22). Every step of the way between those two challenges, Peter stumbled but never completely failed to continue onward. His life proves that God's unconditional love compensates for our conditional affections. No matter what we have done or what we will do, He will never stop caring for us. The challenge for us is to embody this same devotion to the people in our lives. Can we continue loving when the rest of the world stops? Yes. With the empowerment of the Holy Spirit, we can extend the unconditional love to others that He has bestowed upon us.

EXTRA VERSES FOR STUDY OR PRAYER
John 21; 1 & 2 Peter

VERSE OF THE DAY

Know therefore that the LORD your God is God; he is the faithful God, keeping His covenant of love to a thousand generations of those who love Him and keep his commandments.

—Deuteronomy 7:9

PRAYER

Lord, I know I've failed You. Forgive me for my rejection and denial of You. Thank You for loving me unconditionally despite what I do. I know You love me for who I am and not for what I can give You. Free me from the pressure to perform and strive for approval and acceptance. Help me to love You and the people in my life without conditions, limitations, reservations, or qualifications. In Jesus's name, amen.

THINK

_____

_____

_____

PRAY

_____

_____

_____

PRAISE

_____

_____

_____

TO-DO   PRAYER LIST

_____   _____

_____   _____

_____   _____

QUESTIONS FOR DEEPER REFLECTION

1. How would you respond if Jesus asked you, "Do you love Me?" How strong is your faith? Is it strong enough to stand up under intense trials?

_____

_____

_____

2. Is there a relationship in your life where you have stopped loving the other person? How can you love them again?

_____

_____

_____

DAY 21

LOVING INTENTIONALLY

Be careful that you do not forget the Lord.
—Deuteronomy 6:12

"Did you sleep well?" I inquired as I braided Kate's hair.

"You literally just asked me that," she responded in disbelief.

In my mind, I'd questioned her brother since I had just left his room. I suppose I'd checked on him too, and now Kate—twice. Clearly, I was still tired and needed another cup of coffee. I wish I could tell you this was a one-time occurrence, but I have been forgetful recently.

I'm not sure why my brain has been so foggy lately. In my current state, it's not uncommon for me to enter a room and draw a blank about why I was there. Or open the refrigerator in preparation for dinner, only to pause as I attempt to recall the necessary ingredients. Sure, sometimes I'm distracted by the noise in the room—family members, television, or my phone. But more often than not, the racket within my mind disrupts me most.

Am I alone in this struggle? I don't think so. A great deal of research has been conducted in an effort to better understand our society's recent bent toward absent-mindedness. Our brains process 70,000 thoughts a day.[12] Because our brains are so busy, scientists have identified a condition called "the doorway effect." This is a psychological event in which a person forgets something as soon as they enter a

---

12. "You are your Brain," *Healthy Brains* by the Cleveland Clinic, healthybrains.org/brain-facts.

room.[13] Anyone else feel a bit relieved? It's good to know I'm not alone when it comes to walking around aimlessly from room to room!

Other than our busyness, experts have determined one of the most common explanations for forgetfulness is a simple failure to retrieve information. When memories are rarely accessed, they decay over time. The good news is that we can strengthen our memories by regularly recalling events and experiences to ourselves and sharing them with others.[14] I love this advice because God's Word imparts the same wisdom.

SOMETHING TO THINK ABOUT

Forgetfulness is an age-old problem. The Israelites struggled to remember, and we inherited our spiritual amnesia from them. God led His people out of Egypt and through the desert for forty years. Before the Israelites entered the new territory, their leader, Moses, reviewed the history of God's previous care for them. He urged them to be careful not to forget what their eyes had seen or let the truths they witnessed dissipate from their hearts. (See Deuteronomy 4:9.) He implored them to recite their testimonies of God's faithfulness to their children and grandchildren.

Moses encouraged the Israelites to talk about God's Word at home, while walking along the road, before bed at night, and in the morning. (See Deuteronomy 6:7.) It was an invitation to make remembrance an integral part of their daily life. To help them fix their minds on the ways of the Lord, he suggested tying symbols on their hands and binding them to their foreheads. And as if he knew about the "doorway effect," Moses told them to write the laws *"on the doorframes of your houses and on your gates"* (Deuteronomy 6:9)! He knew they would need physical reminders of what God had saved them from, what He expected of them, and what He would provide for them in the new land. This exhortation is boldly reiterated in Deuteronomy 6:12: *"Be careful that you do not forget the LORD."*

13. Charles Brenner and Jeffrey Zacks, "Why Walking Through a Doorway Makes You Forget," *Scientific American*, December 13, 2011.
14. Ryan Daley, Ph.D., et al., "What Happens When We Remember," *Psychology Today*, November 1, 2021, www.psychologytoday.com/us/blog/achievements-the-aging-mind/202111/what-happens-when-we-remember.

However, they *did* forget. That really is the story of the Bible. It is our story too. We fail to remember God's goodness and the magnitude of our sins. We get so distracted by the trappings of this life that we lose sight of Who created the world and Who formed our own unique minds.

The enemy of our souls wants us to live in forgetfulness. Distracting our focus is a tactic of Satan. This is why it is essential for us to follow the Lord's counsel: *"Keep this Book of the Law always on your lips; meditate on it day and night"* (Joshua 1:8). Because when we seek to know God and His Word, His principles and values become the foundations of all we think and do. Through the practice of remembrance, we are compelled to recount and return His love.

Thankfully, we have the Holy Spirit available to teach, counsel, instruct, guide, *and* remind us. So even if you feel a bit scatterbrained, take heart and remember this: *"For the Spirit God gave us does not make us timid, but gives us power, love and self-discipline"* (2 Timothy 1:7). Through His power, we can have clarity and soundness of mind, which enables us to love Him and others well. Thank You, Lord, that while our memories may be short, You have never forgotten us.

EXTRA VERSES FOR STUDY OR PRAYER
Proverbs 15:14; 2 Timothy 1:7

VERSE OF THE DAY
Be careful that you do not forget the LORD.

—Deuteronomy 6:12

PRAYER
Father, forgive me for being so absent-minded. I fail to call to mind Your presence, provision, and the purpose You have for my life. Help me testify of Your goodness and mercy and retell my story so others may begin to recall their testimonies too. Please keep my thoughts fixed on You. Remove any

distractions that threaten to steal attention from You. In Jesus's name, amen.

THINK

_____

_____

_____

PRAY

_____

_____

_____

PRAISE

_____

_____

TO-DO   PRAYER LIST

_____   _____

_____   _____

_____   _____

QUESTIONS FOR DEEPER REFLECTION

1. Are there seasons of life when it seems as if you have forgotten God? What steps can you take to keep your mind focused on His love for you and your love for Him?

_____

_____

_____

2. What typically consumes your thoughts? How can you be more intentional about what you consume mentally? Are there any distractions you can remove? How can you recount and retell the goodness of God in your story to help you remember?

_____

_____

_____

DAY 22

LOVING RESOLUTELY

*No, in all these things we are more than conquerors through
him who loved us. For I am sure that neither death nor life,
nor angels nor rulers, nor things present nor things to come,
nor powers, nor height nor depth, nor anything else
in all creation, will be able to separate us from the love of God
in Christ Jesus our Lord.*
—Romans 8:37–39 (ESV)

My daughter Kate and I were having a Hallmark movie girls' night. One evening, a movie titled *Love Locks* appeared on the screen. As Kate and I chatted about it afterward, I wondered if there was any truth to the fictional story, which was set in Paris, renowned as the *City of Love*. Sure enough, a quick Google search revealed that love locks are a modern tradition practiced in the city on grills, grates, and fences on different bridges over the Seine River. Couples inscribe their names or initials on padlocks, attach them to the railings, and throw the keys into the river. The ritual symbolizes the permanent sealing of the couple's love.

Interestingly, the custom originated in Hungary. The legend dates back to World War I when a woman who lost her lover fixed multiple padlocks on the various bridges where they used to meet. It was her way of expressing that their love was unbreakable.[15] Soon, the

---

15. "The True Story of the Paris Love Lock Bridge," City Wonders, March 9, 2015, citywonders.com/blog/France/Paris/paris-love-lock-bridge-story.

trend caught on and became a practice in other parts of the world. As the custom spread, the City of Love became renowned for it.

Locals and tourists caught on to the craze with such enthusiasm that it caused some serious repercussions. Due to the accumulated weight of the locks, many landmarks began to collapse. The city remedied the unexpected ruin by removing the locks and installing panels on the structures to prevent people from attaching new ones.

Despite these efforts, love locks haven't entirely disappeared from the bridges over the Seine. People continue to discover creative locations to place what they hope will be a permanent display of their love. However, city authorities warn any new locks will likely be removed, breaking what the lovers hoped would be secure.[16]

SOMETHING TO THINK ABOUT

Love locks are a romantic sentiment, aren't they? They serve as a symbol of a union people hope will endure the trials of life. But as we know, many partnerships are separated by distance, unexpected circumstances, and even death. In contrast, we have a secure relationship with God that remains forever. The apostle Paul summarizes this truth beautifully. He declares, "*Who shall separate us from the love of Christ? Shall tribulation, or distress, or persecution, or famine, or nakedness, or danger, or sword?*" (Romans 8:35 ESV).

Scripture tells us that when we receive Christ as Savior, we are sealed with the Holy Spirit. (See Ephesians 1:13.) This sealing is a promise that our salvation is granted now and forever. It is permanent, irrevocable, and secure. As believers, we are marked with God's seal to identify us as His own (see Revelation 7:2–4), guaranteeing His protection over our souls. We can take great comfort in this reality: "*The Lord knows those who are his*" (2 Timothy 2:19).

But even with this knowledge, you've likely felt separated from God at certain times. Perhaps there was a particularly painful trial

16. Emanuella Grinberg, "Paris ends relationship with 'love locks,'" CNN, June 1, 2015, www.cnn.com/travel/article/paris-love-locks-bridges-feat/index.html.

or season of suffering you experienced that put an emotional distance between you and Him. Maybe you even find yourself feeling disconnected today. My friend, while we may move, God never moves.

Rather than locking ourselves to an earthly landmark that will one day fall away, let us link to the firm foundation of God. (See Matthew 7:24–29.) Like Paul, I am also convinced that nothing in this world can overcome His affection. Paul points out, *"If God is for us, who can be against us?"* (Romans 8:31). No matter what happens in life, we can rest assured that the Lord will care for us through it all. We can trust that our destiny is secure. He is the lock, and He holds the key.

EXTRA VERSES FOR STUDY OR PRAYER
Ephesians 1:13–14; Revelation 7:2–4

VERSE OF THE DAY

No, in all these things we are more than conquerors through him who loved us. For I am sure that neither death nor life, nor angels nor rulers, nor things present nor things to come, nor powers, nor height nor depth, nor anything else in all creation, will be able to separate us from the love of God in Christ Jesus our Lord.
—Romans 8:37–39 (esv)

PRAYER

Father, forgive me when I look for security in all the wrong places. I want to fasten myself to You. Thank you for Your love that knows no bounds and keeps me tethered to You. May I rest in the peace of Your promises and cling to You as I grow to know You more. You alone hold me secure. In Jesus's name, amen.

THINK

_____

_____

_____

PRAY

_____

_____

_____

PRAISE

_____

_____

_____

TO-DO

_____

_____

PRAYER LIST

_____

_____

QUESTIONS FOR DEEPER REFLECTION

1. How close does God feel to you? In times of suffering, are you prone to push Him away or pull Him close? How can you move closer to Him today?

_____

_____

_____

2. Do you place your security in people and places, or in the Lord? If you are a believer, how does knowing you are sealed for eternity comfort you? If you are not a believer, would you like that security? If so, turn to the appendix for a prayer to accept Jesus as your Lord and Savior.

_____

_____

_____

DAY 23

LOVING LAVISHLY

If I speak in the tongues of men or of angels, but do not have love, I am only a resounding gong or a clanging cymbal. If I have the gift of prophecy and can fathom all mysteries and all knowledge, and if I have a faith that can move mountains, but do not have love, I am nothing. If I give all I possess to the poor and give over my body to hardship that I may boast, but do not have love, I gain nothing.
—1 Corinthians 13:1–3

Christmas is a big deal around our house. We all love the festivities surrounding the holiday, especially gift-giving. I wake up early every year and fight the crowds to shop on Black Friday. The night before, I scour the sales circulars to make my list and figure out my game plan for the next day. The long lines are worth the money saved—at least that's what I tell Bryan! By the end of the day, my car is usually so packed, I can barely see out the rearview mirror. With my heart full, I head home to unload the goodies in my secret hiding spot.

On Christmas Eve, Bryan and I assemble the presents that haven't been wrapped yet. We've been known to stay up until after midnight to build a dollhouse or secure a basketball goal to surprise the kids. It is one of our greatest joys to watch the excitement on our children's faces when they wake up the next morning to discover what we bought for them.

I always take special care to balance the presents so that I've spent an equal amount on each child and the number of boxes to unwrap seems even. However, we always explain that an item in a small box could be more valuable than an item in a large box. It's important to us that both kids feel lavished with love all year-round, but especially on Christmas.

While we enjoy all the merriment, Jesus, of course, is the greatest gift. I know the real reason for the season is not about the presents but about celebrating His birth. We certainly make an effort to focus on Him during the hustle and bustle of the holiday. But beyond the gold, frankincense, and myrrh the wise men brought to give the Christ child, I'm reminded of the Scripture that tells us, *"Every good and perfect gift is from above"* (James 1:17).

We don't just receive gifts from God on specific dates; we are the recipients of His generosity all year long. God has already given us all we'd ever require: His Son, His Holy Spirit, forgiveness, and eternal life. Even so, He encourages us to ask Him for whatever we need. (See John 15:7.)

SOMETHING TO THINK ABOUT

To explain this concept to His disciples, Jesus taught:

Which of you, if your son asks for bread, will give him a stone? Or if he asks for a fish, will give him a snake? If you, then, though you are evil, know how to give good gifts to your children, how much more will your Father in heaven give good gifts to those who ask him!   —Matthew 7:9–11

In His teaching, Christ explains the heart of the Father. God is not stingy. We don't have to grovel as we present our requests because He is a loving Father who cares. If humans can be generous, imagine how big-hearted God is!

He has given us all special treasures. These are different, *"according to the grace given to each of us"* (Romans 12:6). One is not superior to another. We should treat everyone's talents and abilities, ours included, as valuable to God. They are bestowed upon each person by the Holy Spirit to serve God and enhance the lives of others.

As you seek to identify and utilize what God has blessed you with, make loving God and fellow Christians your inspiration. Spiritual gifts like great faith, acts of dedication, and sacrifice produce very little without love. As believers, we may have different abilities, but we have a common goal: to share what we've been granted so unbelievers will also come to know God and His lavish gifts.

EXTRA VERSES FOR STUDY OR PRAYER
Romans 12; 1 Corinthians 12

VERSE OF THE DAY

If I speak in the tongues of men or of angels, but do not have love, I am only a resounding gong or a clanging cymbal. If I have the gift of prophecy and can fathom all mysteries and all knowledge, and if I have a faith that can move mountains, but do not have love, I am nothing. If I give all I possess to the poor and give over my body to hardship that I may boast, but do not have love, I gain nothing. —1 Corinthians 13:1–3

PRAYER

Lord, thank You for all You've given me in Your Son, the Holy Spirit, and the hope of eternity. Help me to grasp the magnitude of the gifts You have lavished upon me as Your child. Remind me that it was never anything I earned or deserved, but a result of Your generosity to me. Help me to steward what You have given me well and share it cheerfully because it is not about me but always about You and for You. In Jesus's name, amen.

THINK

PRAY

_____
_____
_____

PRAISE

_____
_____
_____

TO-DO   ## PRAYER LIST

_____   _____
_____   _____
_____   _____

QUESTIONS FOR DEEPER REFLECTION

1. Do you view God as your Father and yourself as His child? Have you felt lavished or lacking in love from Him?

_____
_____
_____

2. What steps can you take to share the gifts you've been given?

_____
_____
_____

DAY 24

LOVING OBEDIENTLY

If you love me, keep my commands.
—John 14:15

When my kids were younger, we had a chore chart on the refrigerator where they could earn gold stars for completing their daily responsibilities. At the end of the week, if they had earned ten gold stars, they would receive a reward, which was typically a sweet treat or a new toy. This method of rewarding good behavior worked well for us for their weekly jobs. However, consequences for poor choices were also necessary. We expected immediate obedience when we told our kids to do something. If they didn't respond or misbehaved, they would receive time-out or we would take away an activity they enjoyed for a while.

Then, of course, there were situations that weren't worth the fight. For instance, as a toddler, Will wanted to wear pajamas to church. We simply put his church clothes on over them! Likewise, for a while, Kate did not want to wear shoes, so we just let her go without them. In fact, our church nursery affectionately called her, "Shoeless Kate." Pick your battles, right?

What about you? Are you motivated by rewards and consequences? I have a hunch you are. I certainly am. I'd love a gold star or two to validate my efforts! Parents, teachers, employers, and governments all function with this mentality. If we abide by the rules or laws, there are positive results; if we don't, there are negative outcomes.

This creates an orderly society and helps us know the appropriate way to behave in any given situation.

God set a similar system in place in the garden of Eden. He told Adam not to eat from the Tree of Knowledge of Good and Evil or he would die. (See Genesis 2:17.) God was very clear about the punishment for disobedience. When Adam and Eve disobeyed by eating from the tree, they were banished.

God continued His instructions through Moses in the book of Leviticus. Near the end of this book, God again clearly states the conditions for His blessings and punishment. If the Israelites obeyed, God promised an abundant harvest, peace in the land, increased numbers, and His presence among them. However, if they disobeyed, disaster would follow. It was a very transactional, if-then theology. The Lord proclaimed He would maintain His love to a thousand generations and forgive sin. Yet He would not leave the guilty unpunished, disciplining *"the children and their children for the sin of the parents to the third and fourth generation"* (Exodus 34:7).

By Jesus's time, many people, particularly the Pharisees, looked at the law outlined in the Old Testament the wrong way. They saw it as a means to prosperity in this world and the next. They mistakenly thought observing every statute was the path to earning God's protection and provision. Keeping the law became an end in itself, not the means to fulfill God's command to love.

SOMETHING TO THINK ABOUT

As hard as mankind tried, they could never live perfectly. Jesus was the only One who could. In the ultimate act of obedience, He died on behalf of all humanity and replaced the old covenant with a new one. We are no longer bound by the if-then theology in which our actions earn God's mercy. Jesus's act of love on the cross gave us that grace freely. The transactional approach to living became relational. When we believe in Him, every condition is replaced with His unconditional love.

However, this truth does not free us of responsibility completely. While we cannot earn salvation, our obedience demonstrates that our faith is genuine. If we love God, compliance will naturally follow. But we must be careful not to link dutifulness to immediate reward. We cannot expect ongoing prosperity without any exposure to suffering. If this were the case, good people would always be rich, and struggle would always be a sign of sin.

What we can expect now, through our yielding, is a right relationship with God and the gift of knowing Him. When we trust Him as Savior and Lord, we are given the promise of spending eternity with Him. This is the greatest blessing imaginable. The Bible tells us that we will receive a reward for our faithful service on earth and in heaven. Until then, we do our best to follow God's clear instructions in the Word.

Jesus understood obedience as an extension of love. It not only demonstrates our love through action, obedience also encourages our souls. Jesus taught, *"If you obey me, I will keep loving you, just as my Father keeps loving me, because I have obeyed him"* (John 15:10 CEV). He was clear, *"If you love me, keep my commands"* (John 14:15).

To love Him, we must obey His Word in commitment and conduct. Thankfully, the Holy Spirit can empower us to live out our call to obedience. When we do, we will find life is less complicated and more rewarding.

EXTRA VERSES FOR STUDY OR PRAYER
Exodus 34:6–7; Leviticus 26

VERSE OF THE DAY

If you love me, keep my commands.   —John 14:15

PRAYER

Father, help me to not only hear Your voice, but to obey Your instructions. Remind me of the commands You've already given me. Help me to be more sensitive to Your Spirit's leading. Forgive me for my disobedience and prompt me to respond to You as soon as I hear Your call. Thank You for Your example of obedience even in the midst of immense suffering. In Jesus's name, amen.

THINK

_____

_____

_____

PRAY

_____

_____

_____

PRAISE

_____

_____

_____

TO-DO

_____

_____

_____

PRAYER LIST

_____

_____

_____

QUESTIONS FOR DEEPER REFLECTION

1. In what ways have you been obedient to God's call? In what ways have you been disobedient?

   _____

   _____

   _____

2. What commands has God clearly given you already? Are there any new instructions you feel He is prompting you to follow?

   _____

   _____

   _____

DAY 25

LOVING SACRIFICIALLY

This is how God showed his love among us: He sent his one and only Son into the world that we might live through him. This is love: not that we loved God, but that he loved us and sent his Son as an atoning sacrifice for our sins.
—1 John 4:9–10

Carrying another human being internally for nine months physically affects a woman's body. The scars on our bellies serve as a reminder of the personal physical sacrifice we offered. This offering continues once we bring our babies home. We forfeit many of our needs and desires to care for our kids. In the beginning, we give up our sleep, waking up at all hours of the night at the sound of their cries to rock them, feed them, and change their diapers.

As they grow older, we abdicate our preferences. We forgo our hobbies and pastimes to build with blocks and play dress up. As mothers, we watch cartoons and Disney movies instead of binge-watching Netflix. We cheerfully order Happy Meals for them and take them to playgrounds rather than meeting our friends and having adult conversations at a coffee shop.

Parenting means parting with finances and resources. Moving from a family of two to a family of more stretches our pocketbooks. Our grocery, clothing, and health care bills increase; our home sizes grow to make space for the newest additions. Once the kids are in their teens, our financial planning must now account for multiple drivers and college tuition.

Moreover, motherhood requires us to relinquish our time. To parent our offspring well, we expend countless hours in conversations to discipline, guide, and teach them. We spend long stretches in the car like a taxi driver to transport our kids from one activity to another. And through it all, we worry about them, think about their problems and their futures, and pray for them.

Looking back upon how much we as mothers have given up amazes me. But it's even more impactful to consider how much more we have gained. When I reflect on the privilege and responsibility of being a parent, nothing overwhelms my heart more. I would forfeit my body, sleep, preferences, finances, resources, and time all over again to experience the love I've come to know as a result of becoming a mother. There is no question that the sacrifice has been worth it.

SOMETHING TO THINK ABOUT

The Bible tells the story of Abraham and Sarah, who longed to have a child. Abraham was one hundred years old, and Sarah was ninety when their son Isaac was born. After finally giving these parents the desire of their hearts, God tells Abraham, *"Take your son, your only son, whom you love—Isaac—and go to the region of Moriah. Sacrifice him there as a burnt offering on a mountain I will show you"* (Genesis 22:2).

Scripture records that Abraham got up early the next morning, saddled his donkey, cut enough wood for the burnt offering, and set out for the place God told him about. He told Isaac that God would provide a lamb for the burnt offering. When they reached where God directed him, Abraham built an altar and laid Issac on the wood.

Though ready to complete the deed, an angel of the Lord stopped Abraham. When he looked up, he saw a ram in the thicket. Mercifully, he sacrificed the animal instead of his son. The Lord had provided. (See Genesis 22:13–14.) As a result of Abraham's obedience, he received abundant blessings. God promised Abraham children and grandchildren who would, in turn, bless the whole earth and give protection from his enemies. (See Genesis 12:1–3.)

Notice the parallel between Abraham's willingness to sacrifice his son and the Father's sacrifice of His Son, the Lamb of God, on the cross as a substitute for us. Whereas God stopped Abraham from sacrificing his son, God did not spare Jesus from crucifixion. God sent His only Son to die for us so that we could be spared from the eternal death we deserve and instead receive eternal life.

This act is summarized in this verse: *"For God so loved the world that he gave his one and only Son, that whoever believes in him shall not perish but have eternal life"* (John 3:16). God paid greatly with the life of His Son, the highest price He could pay. Jesus accepted our punishment, took the penalty for our sins, and then offered us the new life He purchased for us. Like Jesus, we must willingly sacrifice our comfort and security so that others might join us in receiving God's love.

EXTRA VERSES FOR STUDY OR PRAYER
Matthew 16:24; John 15:13

VERSE OF THE DAY

This is how God showed his love among us: He sent his one and only Son into the world that we might live through him. This is love: not that we loved God, but that he loved us and sent his Son as an atoning sacrifice for our sins. —1 John 4:9–10

PRAYER

Father, thank You for Your sacrificial love. May I never forget the magnitude of a Father giving up His only Son, and Jesus willingly laying down His life on the cross for me. I want to take up my cross and follow You. Help me to surrender my selfish desires and notice the needs of others. Empower me to sacrificially show them Your love with all that I am. In Jesus's name, amen.

THINK

_____

_____

_____

PRAY

_____

_____

_____

PRAISE

_____

_____

TO-DO   PRAYER LIST

_____   _____

_____   _____

_____   _____

QUESTIONS FOR DEEPER REFLECTION

1. Who has modeled sacrifice in your life? What did they give up for you?

_____

_____

2. Think about what you have a hard time giving up. How can you lay that down to sacrificially love someone?

_____

_____

_____

DAY 26

LOVING YOUR NEIGHBOR

The second is this: "Love your neighbor as yourself."
There is no commandment greater than these.
—Mark 12:31

We were building a home on our farm, and most days, I'd take our two dogs for a walk along the property. One day, a German Shepherd ran through the fields from the neighboring farm to greet us. Soon afterward, a car we weren't familiar with traveled down our gravel driveway. An elderly woman, hardly five foot tall, exited her sedan. "Hello, I'm Doris," the petite powerhouse introduced herself, extending her hand in neighborly welcome. She told us she'd been meaning to stop by to meet us and coming to retrieve her dog, Russell, stopped her excuses.

We later learned she had recently been widowed and managed a farm three times as large as ours. Her children didn't live in the area, so she lived alone with Russell. He continues to visit us almost daily, so as you can imagine, Doris does too. And each time she does, we talk. We love getting to spend time with her. More often than not, she brings baked goods, cuttings from her garden, or a seasonal surprise for the kids. On one particular visit, she brought us a home-made angel food cake. This delicious dessert is her specialty, and she makes this available throughout the year for anyone who is grieving or sick.

My daughter Kate and I wanted to carry on the tradition of making and taking angel food cakes to our neighbors to spread the love, so I asked Doris to teach us. When she arrived in our kitchen, she gave us an angel food cake tin and taught us how to make her recipe, which we now have the honor of sharing ourselves. She didn't just teach us a skill; she taught us how a Christian woman behaves. How to be a good neighbor. We didn't know it, but God gave us our own "angel" right next door.

My family has moved multiple times, and we have not always been as fortunate to have good neighbors like Doris. She and Russell are easy to love. We've lived next to people who have been noisy, nosy, rude, and unfriendly. I imagine you have had many of the same experiences. But God tells us, *"Love your neighbor."* Not just the Dorises or the Fred Rogers in our lives, but everyone.

SOMETHING TO THINK ABOUT

When a man asked Jesus, *"Who is my neighbor?"* (Luke 10:29), Jesus shared the concept of neighborly love in the parable of the good Samaritan. (See Luke 10:30–37.) In the story, a man was traveling on the road from Jerusalem to Jericho when he fell into the hands of robbers. They stripped him of his clothes, beat him, and went away, leaving him half dead. A priest and a Levite were traveling the same road. When they saw the man, they passed by on the other side. But a Samaritan who saw the injured man took pity on him. He bandaged his wounds, put the man on his donkey, and brought him to an inn. The next day, he gave money to the innkeeper and said, *"Look after him ... and when I return, I will reimburse you for any extra expense you may have"* (verse 35).

The robbers in the story treated the wounded man as an object to exploit; the priest and the Levite treated the man as a problem to avoid; and the innkeeper treated him as a customer to serve for a fee. Only the Samaritan treated the injured man as a person to love.

Keep in mind that the Jews considered themselves to be pure descendants of Abraham and considered the Samaritans to be *unclean*, a mixed race due to intermarriage after Israel's exile. As a result, there was deep hatred between the two groups. Understanding this historical context emphasizes the true goodness of the Samaritan's actions.

It also calls us to consider who our neighbor is and what it means to love our neighbor without bias or judgment. If we see a neighbor with a physical, financial, emotional, or spiritual need, we should act to meet that need. Jesus praised the good Samaritan's actions and told us, *"Go and do likewise"* (Luke 10:37).

Who is next to you? Who touches your life on a daily basis? That is your neighbor. How can you show love to them today?

EXTRA VERSES FOR STUDY OR PRAYER
Matthew 19:19; Luke 10:25–37

VERSE OF THE DAY

The second is this: "Love your neighbor as yourself." There is no commandment greater than these. —Mark 12:31

PRAYER

Father, some people are easy to love, but others can be more difficult. Forgive me for not reaching out to my neighbors when I should have. Lead me to know when and how to help the people You have intentionally placed around me. No matter where I go and who I meet, help me to see each individual as a person to love and as an opportunity to fulfill Your command to love my neighbor. In Jesus's name, amen.

THINK

_____

_____

_____

PRAY

_____

_____

_____

PRAISE

_____

_____

_____

TO-DO   ## PRAYER LIST

_____   _____

_____   _____

_____   _____

QUESTIONS FOR DEEPER REFLECTION

1. Considering the story of the Good Samaritan, who has been unneighborly to you? Is there a person who has been a good neighbor to you? How so?

_____

_____

_____

2. How can you be a better neighbor to the people around you? What is one thing you plan to do for the person who lives near you? Consider making an angel food cake. The recipe is in the appendix.

_____

_____

_____

DAY 27

LOVING YOURSELF

*For we are God's handiwork, created in Christ Jesus to do good
works, which God prepared in advance for us to do.*
—Ephesians 2:10

One day when our two children were toddlers, we were enjoying a summer day at the community pool. In the midst of applying sunscreen and adjusting swimmies, an acquaintance approached me. After exchanging pleasantries, she said, "I didn't know you were expecting again." This comment would have been acceptable *if* I was pregnant with my third child; however, I was *not*. Obviously, I was still hanging on to the weight from my previous pregnancies.

This brief interaction left me overheated despite the cooling effects of the pool. I let one person's one-minute comment ruin an entire day. That evening, I rehashed the conversation with my husband. The next morning, I found Ephesians 2:10 written on an index card taped to my bathroom mirror. Bryan had personalized the verse for me: "Rachael, you are God's workmanship, and what a beautiful work He has created." My husband's words were a desperately needed reminder of my inherent worth to him and to God.

Though it is not nearly as crisp and white as it once was, that index card is still taped to my bathroom mirror. I see it every day as I look at my reflection. Some days, like that summer day a decade ago, I need the verse to encourage my heart regarding my physical appearance, especially as my hair begins to gray and my smile lines become more pronounced. But more often than not, I need the verse emotionally and spiritually.

You see, just like I allowed that woman's comment—that I'm still hanging on to and writing about a decade later—to stir up comparison, guilt, insecurity, and shame about my body, I do the same thing when it comes to my personality traits and talents ... or lack thereof. Unlike the Evil Queen in *Snow White*, I am not under any pretense of thinking I'm the fairest of them all. I don't always look in the mirror and admire who or what I see—because I know how often I fall short and how unlovable I really am. So how do we love our neighbor as ourselves, as God commands, when we don't even love ourselves?

SOMETHING TO THINK ABOUT

Self-love isn't what I'm referring to here. That's being focused more on ourselves than on God. In his second letter to Timothy, Paul prophesied about the adverse effects of being a lover of self. (See 2 Timothy 3:1–8.) As the apostle notes in 1 Corinthians 13:4, love *"is not proud."* While we want to keep our gaze on the Lord, we also do not want to have a skewed, unhealthy perspective of ourselves. I'm afraid some of us fail to love ourselves; sometimes, we don't even *like* ourselves. But in between egotistical self-love and self-disdain, there is a healthy balance where we can love ourselves and have the same love for our neighbor.

Genesis 1:27 says we are created in God's image. That means we are a reflection of Him and share many of His characteristics. This provides us with a solid basis for our self-worth. Our significance is not based on possessions, achievements, public acclaim, or physical attractiveness (even in a bathing suit). Because we bear His likeness, we can feel positive about ourselves. Criticizing ourselves is devaluing what God has made and the abilities He has given us.

Since the beginning, when God looked upon all He had created, He said it was *"very good"* (Genesis 1:31). You, too, are a part of God's creation. He is pleased with how He formed you. He created your innermost being and knit you together in your mother's womb; you are "*fearfully and wonderfully made*" (Psalm 139:14). You are His masterpiece. (See Ephesians 2:10.)

If you feel down on yourself and of little value at times, remember God intentionally created you for His purposes. You should have as much respect for yourself as God has for you. I know it's hard to love yourself sometimes. I empathize. I wish I could give you an index card with a personalized version of Ephesians 2:10 to take away the distorted reflection you've been seeing in your proverbial mirror. While I can't give you a card, I hope you can receive these words in your heart and mind: "You are God's workmanship, and what a beautiful work He has created!"

EXTRA VERSES FOR STUDY OR PRAYER

Genesis 1:31; Psalm 139:13–14

VERSE OF THE DAY

For we are God's handiwork, created in Christ Jesus to do good works, which God prepared in advance for us to do.

—Ephesians 2:10

PRAYER

Father, Thank You for creating me in Your image. Remind me of my inherent worth and significance in You. Help me to focus on my God-given identity traits and learn to appreciate who You've uniquely made me. May I see others as people also carefully crafted by You. Forgive me for finding fault with the work of Your hands. In Jesus's name, amen.

THINK

PRAY

_____

_____

PRAISE

_____

_____

TO-DO   PRAYER LIST

_____   _____

_____   _____

_____   _____

QUESTIONS FOR DEEPER REFLECTION

1. What qualities do you not love about yourself? Have someone's words, or something you've done, caused you to feel this way? How does knowing you are created in the image of God change your perception of those qualities?

_____

_____

2. How does knowing you are God's masterpiece change how you feel about yourself and alter your interactions with others? Who in your life needs a reminder that they are also image-bearers of God?

_____

_____

DAY 28

LOVING YOUR FRIENDS

*I in them and you in me—so that they may be brought to
complete unity. Then the world will know that you sent me and
have loved them even as you have loved me.*
—John 17:23

Although Cecelia and I attended the same church, we actually met in the bathroom! We had a sense of recognition when we bumped into each other but had not formally met before.

We continued talking as we walked to our cars. Through our conversation, we realized God had been whispering to each of our hearts separately, and we were feeling led to start a Bible study together. After a few phone calls and meetings over coffee, we agreed on a date and time for the study to begin. This was the inception of our Thursday morning Bible study, called the *morning gathering*.

Each week, around fifty women gather from all over our community. Various ages, races, professions, life stages, and denominations unite for two hours to grow closer to the Lord. The format includes a large group meeting and then breaking into smaller groups to discuss what we've learned. Cecelia and I prayed about a leadership team to help us oversee these groups. God laid five women on our hearts, and they each agreed to facilitate conversation. Our group discussions are lively and engaging because of the unique backgrounds and experiences everyone brings to the table.

Every Thursday, as we set up and brew coffee, our leadership team prays that women will feel welcome, accepted, and loved when they enter the room. Over the years, we have seen the relationships between the women growing closer as they get more comfortable. The women share prayer requests and praises each week, sharing authentically and vulnerably. It's been wonderful to see these ladies encouraging and rallying behind each other in their times of need.

Through this group, I've made many new friends who have become so special to me. Many of the women are young moms carrying babies and chasing toddlers. Others are retired and babysitting grandchildren. Yet when we come together, there is a camaraderie. We share a oneness of heart and soul because of our love for the Lord and His people.

SOMETHING TO THINK ABOUT

Oneness was the heart of Jesus when He walked the earth as Immanuel, *"God with us"* (Matthew 1:23). In the Gospels, we are privy to His interactions with His friends, who were His disciples. These twelve ordinary men had many differences, but they shared common ground—their desire to know Jesus and learn from Him.

Of the twelve, three disciples—Peter, James, and John—seem to have been the closest to Jesus. They were among His earliest disciples and formed His inner circle. Peter, James, and John were present for Jesus's most notable moments of glory and His toughest trials.

Jesus clearly loved this group of motley men. Before He went to the cross, He selected these men to share in His final meal. Even greater, though He knew death was imminent, He spent a good portion of his final moments serving His friends.

In His Upper Room Discourse found in John 13–17, Jesus prays for His disciples and future believers. His prayer for us was that we would be one as Jesus was one with the Father. (See John 17:22.) He prayed, *"That they may be brought to complete unity. Then the world will know that you sent me and have loved them even as you have loved me"* (John 17:23). The most significant prayer Jesus had for His disciples in this critical moment was that they would be unified. His great desire was for these followers to walk in harmony with all believers as an extension of their unity with Him and the Father. Jesus wanted their unity to be a powerful witness to the reality of His love.

We can follow Jesus's example for friendship. He had an inner circle of three and another circle of twelve. Then, He ministered to and fellowshipped with thousands of others. Twice in the Gospels, Jesus is called a *friend of sinners*. (See Matthew 11:19; Luke 7:34.) He never excluded people. He welcomed everyone into a relationship with Him.

The reality is we are all sinful. None of us is perfect, but we are all delightfully different. We don't all have to be the same to become friends. Our distinctions are beautiful, and we can unite even in our diversity. These were some of Jesus's last words for us. Yes, He is our Friend, but He knew we would need one another. Thankfully, He modeled friendship for us. Hear Him call, *"Come, follow me"* (Matthew 4:19). Now, it's up to us to emulate Him.

EXTRA VERSES FOR STUDY OR PRAYER
John 15:14; John 13–17

VERSE OF THE DAY

I in them and you in me—so that they may be brought to complete unity. Then the world will know that you sent me and have loved them even as you have loved me. —John 17:23

PRAYER

Father, thank You for being my Friend. I'm grateful You modeled what it looks like to have friends and how to be a good friend. Help me to be open to new relationships no matter what our differences may be. Give me guidance on how to display Your love to the people You've placed in my life. I pray I follow Your will to be unified, with You at the center of every friendship circle. In Jesus's name, amen.

THINK

_____

_____

_____

PRAY

_____

_____

_____

PRAISE

_____

_____

_____

TO-DO   PRAYER LIST

_____   _____

_____   _____

_____   _____

QUESTIONS FOR DEEPER REFLECTION

1. Who are your closest friends? Do you have trouble making or keeping friends? How can you display love to your friends?

_____

_____

2. Are you helping to unify the body of Christ, the church? Are your friends different than you or very similar? What would it look like for you to create oneness in your community?

_____

_____

DAY 29

LOVING YOUR ENEMIES

*But I say to you who hear, Love your enemies,
do good to those who hate you, bless those who curse you,
pray for those who abuse you.*
—Luke 6:27–28 (ESV)

Who is your worst enemy? Not in a silly superhero versus villain way, but if someone wrote a book about your life, who would be the antagonist? Think about this for a moment. Who has rejected you? Betrayed you? Slandered you? Attacked you? Who has hurt you the most?

It is that person who you are called to love, do good to, bless, and pray for.

Sigh.

Unfortunately, none of us can escape the pain caused by others. Even Jesus, the Savior of the world, endured pain inflicted by those He came to save. Could that be one of the reasons why Jesus chose Judas Iscariot as one of His twelve disciples, despite the fact that He knew this man would betray Him, ultimately leading to His crucifixion? Jesus knew we'd face our own Judases, and He wanted to prepare us to handle those kinds of people. If we are honest, we've been the Judas in a group a time or two, haven't we? And while Judas betrayed Jesus, all the disciples abandoned Him as well, albeit briefly.

So it wasn't just the Pharisees, Sadducees, and the Roman officials who became Jesus's enemies; it was His closest friends. Jesus fully understands what it is like to be rejected, betrayed, slandered, attacked, and hurt. Therefore, when He teaches us to love our enemies during His Sermon on the Mount, He's not speaking theoretically but from personal experience.

Not only does Jesus instruct us to love our enemies, He takes it a step (or a giant leap) further. He challenges us to do good to those who hate us, bless those who curse us, and pray for those who mistreat us. We think, "Jesus, really?" Yes, really.

SOMETHING TO THINK ABOUT

What I love about Jesus is that He doesn't just tell us to do something; He models it to show us how it's done. Being omniscient (all-knowing), Jesus knew that He would soon be betrayed by Judas, disowned by Peter, and deserted by all of the disciples for a time. Yet Jesus chose to humble Himself and show His disciples the full extent of His love by washing their feet. (See John 13:3–5.) When He finished His act of servanthood, He said, "*I have set you an example that you should do as I have done for you*" (John 13:15).

Jesus asks us to follow His example in all areas, including loving our enemies. It's easy to wash someone's feet if you know they'll wash yours in return. Or, in more modern terms, scratch someone's back so they'll scratch yours. Jesus addressed this idea of reciprocity in His Sermon on the Mount.

In Luke 6:32–35, Jesus continued His lesson:

If you love those who love you, what credit is that to you? Even sinners love those who love them. And if you do good to those who are good to you, what credit is that to you? Even sinners do that. And if you lend to those from whom you expect repayment, what credit is that to you? Even sinners lend to sinners, expecting to be repaid in full. But love your enemies, do good to them, and lend to them without expecting to get anything back. Then your reward will be great.

Yes, our task to love our enemies may be great. But our promise to do good to them, expecting nothing in return, is even greater. Can you imagine a world in which everyone reacted with reckless love instead of retaliating with revenge? A world where we no longer give an eye for an eye or a tooth for a tooth but pray for each other and think of ways to help one another? That's what Jesus did for us. We didn't get what we deserved. Instead, *"while we were still sinners, Christ died for us"* (Romans 5:8).

When we are wronged, our natural inclination is to make it right. Thankfully, we serve a supernatural God who can empower us to love as He does when we feel powerless. Trust the Holy Spirit to help you show care to those for whom you do not feel love. Instead of planning vengeance, pray for those who hurt you. This is how we overcome evil with good. What your enemies meant for evil, God will use for good. (See Genesis 50:20.) He is the hero of our story and defeats the devil, the real enemy of our souls, every single time.

EXTRA VERSES FOR STUDY OR PRAYER

Luke 6:27–36; John 13

VERSE OF THE DAY

But I say to you who hear, Love your enemies, do good to those who hate you, bless those who curse you, pray for those who abuse you.   —Luke 6:27–28 (esv)

PRAYER

Father, this command to love my enemies, do good to them, bless them, and pray for them feels impossible on my own. But I know nothing is impossible with You. And so I'm asking that You empower me to do what I cannot do alone. I pray for those who have hurt me most. Help me to forgive and love them as You do. I ask You to bless them and reveal how I may do good to them. In Jesus's name, amen.

THINK

_____

_____

_____

PRAY

_____

_____

_____

PRAISE

_____

_____

_____

TO-DO   PRAYER LIST

_____   _____

_____   _____

_____

QUESTIONS FOR DEEPER REFLECTION

1. Who is your enemy? Who comes first to your mind? In light of
    this devotion, what is your prayer for them? Is there something
    the Holy Spirit is prompting you to do for that person?

_____

_____

_____

2. Is there someone you have wronged who might consider you to
    be their enemy? Consider how you can reach out in love to heal
    that broken relationship.

    _____

    _____

    _____

DAY 30

LOVE ONE ANOTHER

A new command I give you: Love one another. As I have loved
you, so you must love one another. By this everyone will know
that you are my disciples, if you love one another.
—John 13:34–35

I didn't want to see my mom in here again. This was her second cancer diagnosis in seven years. This particular time, I visited with her for a portion of her hospital stay for a stem cell transplant. Despite the dismal situation and surroundings, we had a wonderful time together. Since we don't live in the same community and my brothers and I are all married with children, my mom and I can rarely spend such quality time together alone.

I find it remarkable that while being cooped up in a place we didn't want to be, with a diagnosis we didn't want to face, and while she was receiving treatments that made her feel terrible, we could still enjoy sharing hospital-made meals, working puzzles in a window seat, taking walks in the hallways, making new friends with the nurses, and finding ourselves overcome with laughter.

Being with my mom during this time was a joy. This visit was easy for me to enjoy because I am healthy. I know my mom also treasured our time together although she was being poked and prodded and experiencing pain. She intentionally chose to love the person in front of her no matter how she felt or how bleak the circumstances.

The beauty of what I experienced with my mom wasn't exclusive to us. During my brief stay, I witnessed numerous concerned caregivers with their loved ones. In a hospital filled to the brim with sickness and hopelessness, it was also beaming with love and hope. Through my people-watching, I was privy to family and friends sitting for hours at bedsides, pushing wheelchairs, bringing coffees, delivering flowers, hugging in hallways, praying at tables, sharing meals, holding hands, carrying on conversations, and purchasing gifts. It was impactful for me to see how much we need one another, especially in times of hardship.

SOMETHING TO THINK ABOUT

The phrase *"one another"* in today's verse is derived from the Greek word *allelon*, which means "one another, each other; mutually, reciprocally." This term occurs one hundred times in the New Testament, and it is mostly used in commands on how we are to treat each other.[17] Jesus knew we would need one another, especially once He ascended into heaven. In fact, shortly before His crucifixion, Jesus gave His disciples a new command to *"love one another"* (John 13:34). Jesus was essentially saying that love should be the identifying mark of the Christian community.

The early church was comprised of the first disciples doing their best to obey Jesus's instructions when He was no longer with them. We read their story in the book of Acts. We learn:

> *All the believers were one in heart and mind. No one claimed that any of their possessions was their own, but they shared everything they had. With great power the apostles continued to testify to the resurrection of the Lord Jesus. And God's grace was so powerfully at work in them all that there were no needy persons among them.* —Acts 4:32–34

This last verse grips me. Read it again: *"There were no needy persons among them."* Can you imagine a society where there is no need

---

17. Hilda Scott, "How many one anothers in the Bible?", *The Holy Script*, March 31, 2023, www.theholyscript.com/how-many-one-anothers-in-the-bible.

among us because we, as Christians, care for one another so extravagantly? These early believers exemplified a beautiful model of unity and generosity for us to follow.

Our Christlike treatment of one another displays that we are Jesus's disciples to a watching world. However, how often do people see petty bickering, greed, revenge, callousness, jealousy, and division instead? I'm guilty of all of these things. But may I challenge us today? The world is a hospital for the hurting. People are longing for someone to come alongside and help carry their burdens. Let us meet their needs by helping when it's inconvenient and serving sacrificially. This kind of behavior is hard to do. That is why people notice when you do and know a supernatural source empowers you to do so. Who knows? Maybe loving one another in this countercultural way could welcome someone into the family of God.

EXTRA VERSES FOR STUDY OR PRAYER
Romans 12:10; 1 Peter 5:14

VERSE OF THE DAY

A new command I give you: Love one another. As I have loved you, so you must love one another. By this everyone will know that you are my disciples, if you love one another.

—John 13:34–35

PRAYER

Father, thank You for modeling what it was like to love Your disciples. I'm grateful for the example of the early church. Forgive me for acting in ways contrary to Your nature. Help me to see the burdens in front of me and act to meet those needs with the resources and gifts You have given me. I pray for unity and a spirit of generosity to invade our community. When people are watching me, may they only see You. In Jesus's name, amen.

THINK

_____

_____

PRAY

_____

_____

_____

PRAISE

_____

_____

_____

TO-DO   PRAYER LIST

_____   _____

_____   _____

_____

QUESTIONS FOR DEEPER REFLECTION

1. What kind of behavior do people witness when they watch you?
    Do you think your actions show you are Jesus's disciple?

_____

_____

_____

2. Is there someone God is laying on your heart who might need His love expressed through you today? What steps can you take to become more loving to the people in your life who would follow the model of the generosity and unity of the early church disciples?

_____

_____

_____

DAY 31

DOING EVERYTHING IN LOVE

Do everything in love.
—1 Corinthians 16:14

"There are some unbelievers who are far more loving than some Christians," my pastor asserted one Sunday morning during his sermon. Unfortunately, I agree with that statement. Some people in church have treated me worse than others outside of it. You may have had this experience at some point as well. My pastor's statement causes some serious introspection. Are we loving those around us the way God intended? Are we winning over a lost and dying world? Are unbelievers more endearing than we are?

These are difficult questions to answer and an even loftier ideal to live out. But I pray this thirty-one-day journey has helped simplify what we tend to complicate. We should be winsome in how we behave in hopes that when people interact with us, they encounter Jesus. You've likely heard statements like, "You may be the only Jesus some people ever see," or "You're sharing the only Bible some people ever hear," or "Being with you is the only church some people ever attend." Ultimately, each statement teaches the same lesson: the importance of living, loving, and conducting yourself in a way that saves the unsaved world.

We've been called to be the hands and feet of Jesus so that others come to know the One we have known. God has made Himself known through His Word and dwelt among us through the Messiah. Now, He is revealing Himself through His church. This is the completion and the perfection of God's love, and we have a part to play in the process.

We are circling back to where we started at the beginning of this devotional. After communicating that God is love, John writes, *"No one has ever seen God; if we love one another, God abides in us and his love is perfected in us"* (1 John 4:12 ESV). God is intangible in His fullness and essence. However, we can tangibly see evidence of Him at work through our actions.

As Christians saved by the gospel, we are called to pass on that saving grace to humanity. Love began with God, but He didn't keep it to Himself. He manifested it for us in our Savior, who then embodied love's characteristics on earth. Since God demonstrated love to us, we in turn are called to demonstrate it to mankind. That is God's plan and His mission. Therefore, it is also our purpose.

SOMETHING TO THINK ABOUT

One of the most transformative books I've read to better understand this quest to live out the greatest commandment is *The Five Love Languages* by Dr. Gary Chapman. Through his work as a counselor, Chapman has identified five ways to give and receive love: acts of service, gifts, words of affirmation, physical touch, and quality time.[18]

I appreciate the biblical truth that supports the concepts in Chapman's book. When we consider being winsome, no one has ever been more appealing and magnetic than Jesus. Everything He did in His life on earth was supremely loving. Consider how He modeled these five love languages during His earthly ministry.

+ Acts of service: Jesus washed the disciples' feet, healed the sick, fed people, and sacrificed His life.

+ Gifts: Jesus *is* the gift who keeps on giving. He gave His life willingly, laying it down for us.

18. Gary Chapman, *The 5 Love Languages: The Secret to Love That Lasts* (Chicago: Northfield Publishing, 1992).

+ Words of affirmation: Jesus prayed for people, encouraged them, blessed them, and praised them when they acted in faith.

+ Physical touch: Jesus offered warm embraces, held children, and touched lepers.

+ Quality time: Jesus stepped out of heaven to dwell among mankind. He walked along roads to talk with the disciples, visited synagogues, shared meals, celebrated at weddings, mourned at funerals, and had a lengthy conversation with a Samaritan woman, choosing her to spread the news that He was the Messiah. (See John 4:4–42.)

When we examine how Jesus lived, we realize that we can be like Christ in many of these same ways. Jesus embodied 1 Corinthians 13:4–8. He exemplified love in action. I pray the same will be said of us.

Like God, may love be our motivation and at the heart of everything we do. Let's remember that the most loving thing we can do for anyone is to point them to the *agape* love we've found in Him.

EXTRA VERSES FOR STUDY OR PRAYER
John 3:16; 1 John 4

VERSE OF THE DAY

Do everything in love.   —1 Corinthians 16:14

PRAYER

Father, thank You for loving me. I'm in awe of who You are and how You've displayed Your affection for mankind since the beginning of time. Remind me how much You adore me when I forget. Empower me to exhibit loving actions to the people You've placed in my life. Mold me more into Your likeness, so that an encounter with me is an encounter with You. I pray my life is characterized by love because I know the One who loved me first. In Jesus's name, amen.

THINK

PRAY

PRAISE

TO-DO

PRAYER LIST

QUESTIONS FOR DEEPER REFLECTION

1. What has been your experience with believers versus nonbelievers? Which group is most winsome in your opinion? Now consider which category you fall into. When people see you, do they see Christ in you? When people hear you, are they hearing words that draw them near to God or would it push them away?

---

2. How can you mimic the behaviors of Jesus to show His love through the five love languages? Is there something you can do for someone that communicates that you know the Source of love? What will you do to make His love known?

_____

_____

_____

APPENDIX

If you have never prayed to God for salvation, I encourage you to do so now.

SALVATION PRAYER

Father, I recognize my need for a Savior. I believe in Your Son, Jesus Christ, and acknowledge Him as Lord. I confess my sins, ask for Your forgiveness, and trust in Jesus's sacrifice on the cross on my behalf. I invite You into my life and surrender my will to Yours. I accept the gift of salvation that comes through faith in You and desire to follow You wholeheartedly. I want to live according to Your Word and the guidance of the Holy Spirit. Thank You for Your grace, mercy, and love. May I grow in my relationship with You, obeying completely, loving fully, and living faithfully. In Jesus's name, amen.

DORIS'S ANGEL FOOD CAKE RECIPE

Ingredients

1 cup sifted White Lily plain flour
7/8 cup sugar, plus 3/4 cup sugar
1 1/2 cups egg whites (from 9-10 eggs, approximately)
1 1/2 tsp. cream of tartar
1/4 tsp. salt
1 1/2 tsp. vanilla
1 tsp. almond extract

Directions

Let eggs sit out of the refrigerator for 30 to 45 minutes before starting the cake. Preheat the oven to 375 degrees. Measure and sift together flour and 7/8 cup sugar three times. Set aside. In a large stainless steel or glass mixing bowl, measure egg whites, cream of tartar, salt, vanilla, and almond extract. Gradually beat egg white mixture until frothy, and then increase the speed of the mixer and add 3/4 cup sugar about 2 tablespoons at a time. Continue beating until the meringue holds stiff peaks. Gradually scatter in 3 to 4 heaping tablespoons of the flour-sugar mixture. Continue this process with the remainder of the sugar and flour. Push batter into an ungreased 10-inch tube pan. Bake for 30 to 32 minutes. Upon removing the cake from the oven, immediately invert it and let it hang until completely cold. To release the cake from the pan, take a table knife with a rounded end and go around the sides and tube. Place an 11- to 12-inch plate over the pan and give a quick shake to release the cake. Flip it over and enjoy!

ABOUT THE AUTHOR

Rachael Adams was born and raised in a small Kentucky lake town. After she married her college sweetheart, Bryan, he moved there with her. Together, they run a family business and live on a farm with their two children, Will and Kate, and doodle dogs, Buster and Penny. Rachael spends her days taking care of their farm and home. When she isn't doing something with or for her family, she loves getting together with friends, cooking, taking walks, and reading Christian nonfiction. Rachael is also active in women's ministry at her local church.

She began *The Love Offering* podcast in January 2019. Each week, she interviews guests who are loving people well with the gifts they have been given and living out their faith in practical ways. In October 2020, Rachael began *The Love Offering* blog series. Every Thursday, she publishes stories from guest writers about how they have been loved well or have loved others well to simplify living out the greatest commandments.

Rachael is also a regular contributor to the Salem Web Network, which includes iBelieve, Crosswalk, Your Daily Bible Verse, and Christianity.com. She received her Bachelor of Arts from Transylvania University.

Through her own experience and the conversations she's had, Rachael realized that many Christian women doubt what they have to offer. She wrote a devotional entitled *A Little Goes a Long Way: 52 Days to a Significant Life*. Published in 2022, it became a No. 1 Amazon bestseller in the Christian Devotional category. Rachael believes small acts done with great love can have an enormous impact in God's hands.

Rachael has created the *Everyday Prayers for Love* "Love Notes from God" Scripture cards as a gift to you. Take a picture of this QR code to receive your notes or visit rachaelkadams.com/free.

Connect with Rachael by visiting:

rachaelkadams.com

www.facebook.com/rachaeladamsauthor

www.instagram.com/rachaeladamsauthor